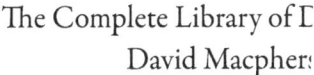

The Complete Library of [
David Macpher[

The Complete Library of Disposable Art
Copyright 2022 and 2024 David Macpherson
All rights reserved
Many of these articles originally appeared in the Worcester Magazine from 2020 to 2024. Thanks once again to Victor Infante and Margaret Smith, two wonderful editors.

The image on the cover is public domain and was available from the Library of Congress.

The Library of Disposable Art Volume One was published in 2022, which had half of what is published here.

macphersondavid607@gmail.com

100pagedash.wordpress.com

On facebook David's group is Dave Macpherson is a Writing Stuff.

Instagram DavidScottMacpherson

Greetings

From February 2020 to July 2024 I wrote a monthly column for the Worcester Magazine. It was about all the stupid things we keep around even though they probably should be tossed. What do we value? What do we want to see on a shelf every day before heading off to work? That is the Library of Disposable Art and I had a blast putting these out.

The column only ended because I found myself tapped out. I liked writing them, but they were getting more challenging to come up with and to stick the landing. One day I looked at the half finished column and realized there was nothing else to write. My editor, Margaret Smith, was understanding.

This book is a collection of all the articles published over those four plus years. There are also several that were not published. Margaret and the initial editor, Victor Infante, would choose to pass on a few. But I wrote them and I am reasonably happy with them, so they will be here.

Thank you for picking this up. It was fun to write and I am always happy to share my work with you.

David
November, 2024

One: Coloring Books

Welcome to the Library of Disposable Art. We are the collection of art that was never meant to be seen or contemplated for more than a glance, like comic strips. It includes things that were never meant to be art, but people love it and keep it all the same, like beer bottles.

Today, I would like to start with the best example of disposable art, the coloring book. Let me clarify, up until ten years ago, the coloring book was in the land of "for kids." We got to give Cousin Mary's son a present when we visit, let's get him a coloring book. Kids like coloring.

We should talk of the adult coloring book and its goal of mindfulness. But if you look at a completed page done by an overstressed forty year old accountant living in Millbury, every section is meticulous and perfectly ordered. That might be nice to calm his frayed psyche, but really, where the hell is the fun in that? Where are the messy smudges and crossed over mistakes? No. Let's stick to coloring books for children.

First question, why do we think that all kids like coloring? We make them color. But do they like it? Of course the way we want them to color is too specific to be fun. Color in the lines. You have to be careful to use the right color and to stay in the marked off areas. School psychologists will wonder what's wrong with you if you scribble with abandon.

Coloring books are not about a finished work. It is a process. You don't look back at the coloring book you have attacked and contemplate it for years to come. As soon as all the pages are filled with crayon trails, then that coloring book is finished. There is no reason to keep it. Toss it out. It is full. Time to get another coloring book to draw on and forget. Coloring books are a temporary fix.

We parents might be impressed with our toddler's first completed page of color and cacophony. We give them a big kiss and stick it to the fridge door with a magnet. The Fridge Door, the child's first art museum. But then soon enough, those coloring book masterpieces are replaced with the menu to the Chinese restaurant that delivers, which is a different kind of disposable art. We love what the little ones do, but after a while, it's just color inside and out of the lines.

And what coloring books do we give them? That doesn't help. Superman. Scooby Doo. Barbie. Bratz. Care Bears. Snoopy. Happy Days. Ghostbusters. Transformers. The things we think they like. We saw Timmy watch Ben 10, he must want to push a crayon over his likeness. It is the facsimile of enjoyable pastimes.

How often did you get a coloring book when you were home sick from school?

It's a throw away. It is a killer of an icy snow day. Kids can be so proud of the Jackson Pollack explosion they put on the line drawing of Garfield and Odie. But they will still turn the page and color the next one. And the next after that. Coloring is a volume activity.

Now I collect a bunch of disposable art. I have original comic book art. I have art that was made for children's books and comic strips. In the case of comic strip art, I love the idea that all of this beautifully detailed work was made just to be reproduced in the newspaper once and only once. I used to spend a good deal of time loitering on EBay, looking for the best bargains for this type of forgotten creation.

But in my collection, the thing that has pride of place are the original art from coloring books. I love having them. They are not pretty things. They are just the pen and ink outline of the action that will be filled in by the kids at home. They are simple things. I have original art from Little Lulu, Blondie and I Love Lucy. I stare at my Fantastic Four coloring book art. I even have all the art for a coloring book that was to teach kids how to be safe on the playground. Of course, the best way to teach kids these rules is to have an anthropomorphic moose and his pals play and cavort. There is no plot, no sequential momentum in these books. It is snapshots of a story that does not fit together.

My wife thinks I'm crazy. She can't understand why I would want these things.

I love the idea of coloring book art. The original art. An artist spent hours or days creating pages of art that was meant to be defaced. They create just enough for the four year old to take over. "Don't worry, I got it from here."

What an exciting thing for an artist to contemplate. They are the inspiration for a thousand interpretations. No finished coloring book page is like any other of the same page. Everything is original. Every page of Strawberry Shortcake playing with her friends is a chance to create something amazing, something with colors we should not expect. Art that ignores lines and rules is the art that we might get a chance to create while killing time during a rainy summer's day or anxiously waiting in the front room of the doctor's office.

Two: Community Theater Programs

What is the difference between memento and artwork?

While looking for something else in my teeming attic of doom, I found a small pile of programs to plays I attended. I must have kept them. Why would I do that?

There are around forty or fifty of them. They start around 1997, when I lived in Somerville, and go towards 2007 or so, when I was married and living in Worcester. I have continued to see theater, I just stopped bothering holding onto the folded piece of paper they gave me when I entered the black box performance space.

These are simple objects. Most are double sided xeroxes made late at night at Kinkos (I really miss the 24 hour copy shops). Most have no illustrations on the cover. They are just pretty fonts discovered on an early version of Word. Some have simple line drawings. Like the cover for the Hovery Players production of the Nerd. We see an illustration of a guy in suspenders sitting on a giant roll of toilet paper. I am sure this is somehow explained in the play. Or maybe not. Maybe someone just thought this looked funny.

These are hastily made pamphlets given out when you enter the play. They are timekillers to look at while you wait for something to start happening. They are prompts for memory. They focus me to remember what the play was, what I was at the time.

There is the neon yellow program for K&K Productions of The Trial of the Catonsville Nine. It was performed at WAG, which is now the Sprinkler Factory. I remember there were no stage lights, so everything was performed with the usual overhead lighting. Where I stood in the back, I noticed someone had left a copy of the play lying about. As the actors performed their lines, I followed along, noting when they messed up a word or reversed a line. This is a memory I did not have a minute before. Looking at the seventeen year old program allowed me to recall that.

That program has pictures and bios of each of the performers. There is a headshot of Mike Duffy, who played the judge. He was an amazing folk singer. I saw him a lot and I loved hearing him every time. He passed away in 2005. I don't know when was the last time I thought of him.

There is the cheaply made program for WPI's production of Return to Forbidden Planet. It was a silly play melding Shakespeare's The Tempest with the old flick Forbidden Planet, all with fifties do-wop songs. I remember liking the robot on roller skates. The actor was having a hard time staying upright through her solos. I didn't want to go by myself, so I talked two friends into going with me. They didn't know each other. They spent the entire play whispering to each other and tentatively holding hands. After the play they decided to go for a drink, I think they forgot to invite me. They started a short, but memorable relationship that evening. I wonder what they recall of the play.

The cover to the playbill for Stageloft's production of Dirty Work at the Cross Roads, doesn't have the play's title on it. You have to go into the program to find out what you are seeing. My wife and I, just married, went to see it. It was an old 100 year old melodrama with a Snidely Whiplash bad guy and a damsel tied to the tracks. They handed out popcorn with the programs and encouraged us to throw popcorn at the bad guy and shout hurrah when the hero appears. The popcorn is gone, the program remains.

There are many other pieces of paper that tell stories not written by any playwright. I Hate Hamlet. The Smell of the Kill. Black Coffee. Escape Artists Don't Bake Brownies. Black Mariah. You're a Good Man Charlie Brown. 42nd Street. The Skin of Our Teeth. Roadside America. Some of these have strong memories. Some of these are just words I typed out for you.

The jury is out if this is disposable art, or just things that are disposable. Can programs for community theater make the leap up to art? I'm not quite sure, but they do for me what good art can: they elicit emotion, they make me think of long gone friends and the fleeting joy of entertainment.

All the programs and concert ticket stubs that we keep in shoeboxes. They might not be art. But they let us recall the art we once were.

Three: Video Cassette Box

The last VCR was manufactured in 2016. That means there are still VCRs out there ready to take care of all your video cassette needs. But there is a finite number that one can actually use. The amount of VCRs will only diminish.

But what is the good of them now that they have crashed right into the wall of obsolescence?

For the most part, you will not be able to watch the videos that you have in a box in the closet. If you want to watch Die Hard, then you can watch it on DVD or whatever streaming service has it. I do know that some rare cult movies are only available on VHS and some serious lovers of obscure horror films will spend some good money for such a treasure. But that is not the usual route.

You can still buy them at That's Entertainment. At Jelly's. At Savers. They do not take pride of place at the Salvation Army any more, but they are for the picking. A dollar. Maybe fifty cents. This is not high end shopping. But they are given space in the stores, so that means someone is buying them.

But I still get stuck on the issue that hardly anyone I know can play the things. It has gone the way of the BetaMax, the Super 8 home movie, photographic slides, and the passenger pigeon. So what is there to do with the VHS cassette?

I went to That's Entertainment today to look at such things as video tapes. They had a small box underneath a table laden with comic books. There was a variety of movies that most of us would not be able to watch. Rebel Rousers. The Godfather. The Day of the Daleks. The Mummy's Tomb. Gone With the Wind. Planet of the Spiders. The Hunchback of Notre Dame, The Terror. The Evil of Frankenstein. Faulty Towers. Once Upon a Time in China. Doctor Who: Robot. Hoosiers.

They are not something I can watch. But I can look at them as art. Why shouldn't we think of the covers and the back copy singing the praises of this movie as art? It is art of the hard sell. Plop your three bucks down to rent me, buddy.

I remember, when I was a kid and the land was lousy with video stores, it was sometimes more fun looking at the covers then it was to actually watch the one that was picked. I could go to the cult movie section and be amused by the cover art and the desperate tag lines. I could be holding the video tape box for Class of Nuke Em High and know that this piece of folded hard cardboard had more artistic validity then the movie it encased. Best just to hold the boxes and imagine what wonders the movie might entail. And that cinematic day dream is what good art tries to do.

I remember going into the old Starship Video on Park Avenue and just wandering and then stop and stare and wander some more. That was the same type of walk I would do in an art museum. Instead of museum guards asking me to not lean in so close, there would be annoyed cashiers wondering if I was I going to rent any movie or not.

I am sure there is someone who collects these boxes. Maybe collapse them into two dimensions and place them in mylar sleeves, to protect their value. No one can harm your mint copy of the box for Maniac Cop II.

I had a book a while back that celebrated the joy of video cassette box art. The book was The Portable Grindhouse: The Lost Art of the VHS Box. I bought it maybe ten years ago at That's Entertainment (a local epicenter for disposable art). One page was the front of a horror movie box from the eighties. Turning the page, you will see the back of the box, where all the huckster prose lingered to sell you on this one, this great horror.

I wish I could go into greater detail on the lurid joys found in that book, but I don't have it anymore. A few years after I picked it up, I found out an old school friend was sick. Tommy and I spent days and weeks and years of our youth haunting video stores looking for the best horror movies. Then we would go to one of our apartments and stay up all night watching these transvestites. We knew even then that the covers were always better than the reality when you pressed play.

When I heard of his cancer, I sent him the book with a note reminding him of all the videos we survived. He got back to me to thank me. He loved being reminded of these old movies, these old friends.

When he passed away I was unable to make it down to New York for the funeral. I don't know what happened to that book I sent him. Who knows. Things get lost. Things get donated or tossed out. All those things get in the way of moving on.

In his honor, on the day of his funeral, I stayed up through the night watching lame, awful horror movies. The only thing that was wrong with that tribute was that none of the movies were on VHS. None were wrapped in their colorful jacket of cardboard.

Four. Orphan Store Signs

I put out an ebook of a project I did during the summer of 2018. It was called Orphan Store Signs. I documented all the orphan store signs I could find throughout Worcester County. I found over a hundred and fifty of them and wrote about each of them.

What is an orphan store sign? I am so glad you asked. I think I came up with the term, though I am not quite sure. Orphan store signs are the signs to a business that is no longer. The sign is there, but the shop is closed for good or has moved or for the last three years is just closed temporarily for renovations.

I walked around Worcester and Fitchburg and Gardner and Northbridge and all the other towns with partially filled Main Street storefronts. Walking down these streets is like looking into the past. There is the Weintraub's Jewish Delicatessen sign like it is still ready to serve a bowl of matza ball soup. But it is not. Just the sign, telling little lies.

It was kind of profound walking around and making note of all these bankrupt dreams. When I started, I thought it would be a lark. I would get some good walking in and find out about all those Closed for Good shops. But as I continued through the weeks, I was taken with sadness.

I was hassled by a caretaker for a bunch of stores in Grafton. I told him I was just looking around. He said there was nothing to look at. All the places were gone and should be to. There was a flood and all the shops were deemed unsafe for occupancy. The signs still remained. Like an echo of a successful past.

I did that a year and a half ago. Now that I am writing about all these types of disposable

Art, my mind went to orphan store signs. The hope I kept was that many of these signs are gone and thriving businesses have taken over. This has happened with the orphan signs of the Blackstone Pub and the

Canal Restaurant. Those signs have been replaced with the Rock Bar and Russo's, respectively.

So, last Monday, I decided to tool around the town and see if there are still some of the same orphan store signs from a year and a half ago.

And the sad thing is, many of them still are there. They represent nothing but the sign themselves. They are the art of remembering places we might never have gone to.

Right in downtown on Main Street in the giant yellow sign for the Great Wall Chinese Restaurant. The sign goes up several stories and is quite a sight. The restaurant has been gone for several years.

Ten feet above the street on Millbury Street is a lovely oval sign for Ciborowski Insurance Agency. I can't tell when they ended business but it has been a long time. A friend of mine has worked across the street from the sign for over a decade and has never noticed it. It's just part of the scenery we scan right over.

Still on Millbury Street we have the two signs that announce Meservey's Harding Rock Cafe. The word cafe is by itself in the larger yellow sign. There is space underneath that might be where the specials of the week were listed, or if they had a band playing the hits of the day.

I look at the sign for the Ethiopian Dream Center and wonder what amazing things happened there. Or at least, what amazing things did they try to have happen there.

When driving on 290, you can see a sign painted on a brick wall that announces the Pro-Vision Golf Performance Studio. "Learn What the Pros Know. The Numbers Simply Do Not Lie."

And let's not even talk about the yards of signage for Irish Times.

All of these signs are a reminder of hard work and bad luck. Talismans of broken hopes and scattered bands of once close co-workers. Every sign you walk under is a piece of unspoken symbolism.

On Harding Street is a beautiful sign that is also a mural and it is one of my favorite pieces of street art in all of Worcester. I think it was made for the former tattoo shop Secret Society. The word tattoo is a riot of color. There is an Illuminati eye and the words "Modern, Sterile, Electric." There are flowers and tentacles. It is an arresting piece of art and I think it is for Secret Society. But I do not know. I am happy to see it still, but also it is too bad that it has not been replaced with new signs of current business, of new art. Art that speaks of the present.

We are always looking at the past.

Five. Beer Cans

Okay now, it's time to go to the art museum. Get ready to see a lot of art. Be prepared to be overwhelmed and thrown into shut down through sensory overload. See trends and head scratchers. That much art, you will want to scurry home and have a nice beer to calm your nerves. Well, you are in luck, because the art museum for today's field trip is at Friendly's Discount Liquor Store in Whitinsville.

Seeing art at a liquor store is a nice alternative to the expected art museum. There is no admission fee. You are allowed to touch the art, just not drink it (until purchased). You are also expected to make a stop at the gift shop (or register) and take something home. Having so much art, so much product, for you to experience, you should not be cheap and you ought to buy yourself some fine art, or at least a six pack.

When I was just a young drinker, there was not a lot of choices for beer at the store. You had the Milwaukee School of Pilsner Art and that was about it. And the cans were nothing exciting to look at or contemplate.

We are in a renaissance for beer currently. There are many small breweries, some right in town, making a wide variety of beer. And their cans and bottles are decorated with witty titles and striking visuals. Isn't it a fact that one of the side effects of the Renaissance was a focus on the arts? Well the beer can art gets that same bump.

It is like every row at the liquor store is another gallery at a museum. So much to look at. They say when you are in the market to buy fine art that you should only purchase something you are dreaming about and realize you can't live without. Isn't that the same thought process when we go and buy a half case of IPA?

Let's walk around the galleries and see what moves us. Please be quiet, or the docent who is currently removing post-date beer from the shelves, might ask us to keep it down, or they might ask for our ID. You never know.

THE COMPLETE LIBRARY OF DISPOSABLE ART 15

We can start with the fine line cartoony label for Flying Dream Brewing Company's The Nightmare After Christmas. The fancy lettering informs us it is a Russian Imperial Stout.

Down a shelf and we have the good girl art of Becky Likes the Smell, a double IPA. The good girl, obviously named Becky, has a full sleeve of tattoos and is giving us a sneer.

A few beers away is a beautiful can practically radiating like a lava lamp. The beer is Charms & Hexes. There are abstract shapes that must mean something. We must stare at it longer to decipher its meaning. Art is never easy to understand.

The beer can art for Wizard Burial Ground: Bourbon Barrel Aged Quadrupel Ale is like something that was airbrushed on a 1970s van. It has wizards and it is groovy.

On to another shelf we see all the different colorful cans for the Prairie Artisan Ales. These are very distinctive in name and in image. I like these very bright, cartoony cans. You see one can from this brewery and you can always identify which is theirs. It's like going into a gallery that has an exhibition of just one artist. The same is true of the shelf with the Prairie beers. The images have a Looney Tune Cartoon feel. There are characters with eyes bulging out and pumpkins checking their twitter feed. The names are great too: Apricot Funk, Bomb, Vape Tricks. It's like potable underground comix.

For more serious art, you might want to cross the aisle and check out the beer from Dieu du Ciel. They are French Canadian, so you know they got class. The labels to the bottles have a sense of dread. There is a German Expression vibe going on with this art. It is not for the faint hearted, bucko. And all the beer has French names, so that must make it important. Ah, the pretensions of art reach all the way to the beer section.

I have no idea what the beers taste of, but just looking at all these beer cans and bottle labels will make one drunk and unable to drive for at least two hours.

It is art. It gives off the art hangover just like going to a museum.

And we take the art home and we break into its top and we drink what we find inside and are very happy. But what do we do with the can? We can collect it. Put it in the basement with all the other beer cans. But no. We toss it. We are expected to. Hell, there is a deposit on all these works of art. We are not expected to keep it. Beer never lasts. That is true even for the art that wraps around it.

Six: Wheaties Boxes

In the sports section of the great collectible shop, That's Entertainment, I found a dozen Wheaties boxes for sale. Yes, for three dollars, you can take one of these bad boys home. They are all in fine shape, collapsed to form a card. There is no cereal with it. It is just the box.

Wheaties started as an accident in a lab, as most breakfast foods are. In 1921, some one spilled wheat bran mixture onto a hot stove and flakes showed up. Soon, Wheaties was for sale with that orange box. In the 1930s, the brand tied itself on to sports. It was the big name for sports and bran cereal. Eat your Wheaties. The Breakfast of Champions. Eat this and you will be the best intramural softball player that has ever been in right field.

Boxes always had a popular, successful sports figure on the box. It was a big deal to get on the Wheaties box. Now, not so much. A 2014 Washington Post article stated that Wheaties has lost 80% of market share in ten years. I don't even notice it when I walk down the cereal aisle to do my weekly shopping.

The boxes for sale at That's E seem to be from the late 90s. There is a Mark McGuire dinging 70 home runs. I think that Mark didn't eat his Wheaties to get to that number of homeruns. I think he used another type of breakfast of champions.

A few of them showed the work of Leroy Neiman. He was a very popular artist who drew painted athletes in a very distinctive, splotchy way. I remember being told how great his art was. I never bought it. Here there is a Neiman painting of Walter Paton. It looks like an athlete ran through a paint store and was smeared with samples.

That's the thing with collectable items, especially disposable items that are now told they have value, either you think they are totally cool or you wonder what the hell is wrong with the person who collected this stuff?

Older boxes of Wheaties are worth a good deal of money. And the ones from the forties and fifties have a very cool graphic quality. That's a nice way of saying, they look pretty neat.

But these newer ones. These ones are just cereal boxes without the thing that makes them worthwhile, the cereal.

Was this someone who heard that Wheaties boxes were some coin, so hoarded them, dreaming of future wealth. Oh, I know we can't pay the heating bill, but just you wait until I sell my Wheaties boxes, then we will be rolling in it.

Maybe I am being too harsh. Maybe someone loved these things. These pieces of cardboard.

Going through a memorabilia shop is an invitation to mystery. You never know what you will find. And you will never understand why someone went out of their way to save them for all these years.

It can drive a person crazy to think of it. It can make someone slightly peckish. Might I recommend a breakfast cereal? You will feel like a champion.

Seven: The Penny

I have a penny collection. I don't know where it is. It's kind of small. It was one of those little portfolios that had indentations so you can put the coins in.

The idea for this wee grouping was that I would have one penny from each year. I was going to have a century of pennies. Each penny has the year it was minted.

The other part of the collection was that all the pennies were to be found in everyday transactions. I was not to purchase from a coin dealer. I just had to get them from the change I was given, from the "leave a penny - take a penny" dishes by the cash register, on the ground, in the change jar in the kitchen.

All the pennies were to be found in the wild.

I think this little project came about when I emptied my pockets filled with keys, coins, wadded tissues and whatever detritus nestled in there (my wife has said that I am the boy with the frog in his pocket) and discovered a few old pennies. One was from the seventies. Another was 1969. Then I noticed a penny from 1946.

I was shocked. There was a lot of hard living right there resting in my palm So, for a few years, I was determined to get a penny from every year. I think the earliest penny I got was from the 1920s.

It was amazing to see how the humble penny had changed. From heavy dark metal of the 1940s to the shiny pliable penny of 2002. The older ones seemed more valuable. Though, point of fact, they still were just a cent.

I never finished the collection. Hell, I don't even know where they are. I hope I didn't sacrifice them to the false god of CoinStar, one of those days I was feeling poor and thrifty. I think it's been a decade since I found a coin that could be added to the collection.

But I think of those stout little guys often. I can hold a penny from 1943 pinched between my fingers and wonder on the long history it has had.

Did kids gamble with it, pitching it up against the wall?

Was it thrown into a cup to help the war effort?

Was it collected with other like minded coins so that the ragged man can get a room, with a clean bed, for the night?

Was it pin money for a housewife?

Was it thrown up and the air as someone shouted "heads."

Was it picked up lucky?

How many comic books did it help purchase?

How many times was it used to buy some penny candy?

How many times was it thrown into a dirty coffee cup sitting in front of a bearded man holding a cardboard sign asking for change?

How many pairs of penny loafers was it a part of?

All of these coins have a long life. They are worn and beautiful. This century of pennies has a long story to tell us.

This penny has a history that is rich and valuable. And it is worth, almost, nothing.

Update: *This column is a little bothersome for me. It was based on an old performance poem I used to do. I changed it enough to feel like I was creating something new. But in the time I wrote it to when it was published, six months had passed. In that time, I was introduced to a terrific singer-songwriter, Guy Clark. He is worth discovering. While I was getting into his catalog, I listened to his song, "Indian Head Penny." That song does the same thing I do in the column, only better. It is awesome. I planned to tell Victor not to use this column, but then I found out that it was already published. Oh well. So, read this column and then listen to Clark's song. You can compare and contrast the two. Write two to three pages, make sure you double space. - David*

EIght: T-Shirt

It was one of those weeks where I probably should have done a few large loads of laundry, because the shelves were getting a little thin on clean clothes. I reached up and pulled out one of the few remaining t-shirts. It was a plain tee, a nice golden rod yellow. I didn't know I had a plain tee of this color, but that was fine. I put it on and went about my day.

It was a few hours later that I noticed something was off with the shirt. It seemed that I got something smudged on it. This is not a rare occurrence. I am a sloppy eater. Food stains on my shirt is just an indication that I liked the meal. On closer inspection, I realized that it wasn't a smudge, but a faded image. I looked hard at it and saw the faint black ink image of a ladybug.

A ladybug! I remember this t-shirt.

We had gone to an art gallery up in Portsmouth. There were some cool prints done with linotype (I don't know what that is, just saying) of animals but done in an 8 Bit retro video game style. In addition to the prints, the artist put some of the images on t-shirts. I bought the ladybug shirt for something like twenty dollars.

The question is, was it just a shirt or was I wearing art? I suppose that for the most part it was something to wear, but I liked the image, I liked the memory of the time in the gallery. I guess it was both things.

But there is an issue if you are washing your art every few weeks after wear. If I wore that shirt 25 times, then it was thrown into the washer that many times.

I guess it was fading from the minute I got it. It stayed in the closet for some time and then it was out the other day and the image is just a ghost. A shadow. No one knows, but me, that hidden in the spaces in the cloth is a cool piece of art. Everyone else will think it is a dirty shirt and I should know better to wear it. It's not a smudge! It's art!

I also have a t-shirt where Tom Waits used to cavort. I picked the shirt up at a Record Store Day seven years ago. It was a gray shirt with a strong graphic of Tom Waits and guitar leaping in front of a stack of amps. You can tell this was a favorite shirt because it has been washed to a tabula rasa. There are dark, unfocused things on the shirt. I know what they are. I still love the image; the image that I can hardly make out. It is a gallery for one.

There are a lot of broken canvases in my shirt shelf. There are the shirts with busted seems that I can't wear but I cannot bear to toss them out. The shirts so faded no one knows what once was on the front. The shirts that don't fit because time and age shrinks them (I will say that instead of the fact that I ain't the beanpole I once was.)

But this is private. T-Shirts are a portal to a time and place. They are so dear that no one will understand your devotion to it. It isn't what the shirt is, it is what happened when it was worn.

This column was written in the dining room, wearing a 19 year old t-shirt. I got it as part of a wedding party. I was honored to be the best man. I got this light gray shirt with a graphic design of a sailboat on the back. It is nothing special. It is very thin in spots. I love it to pieces. And I am sure that when it is in pieces, I will treasure it all the more.

Update: *This was aided by the assistance of my old friend Foster. He shows up in another article, giving me good advice.* I still wear those two t-shirt. I wore the Tom Waits shirt yesterday and got a few hard stares. Was there an image on the shirt? What the hell am I seeing?

Nine The Shredded

Here is the thing with disposable art, sometimes it is disposable not because it isn't wonderful to look at and hold, but because the creator thinks that it should be destroyed. He makes it disposable.

In Franz Kafka's last will, he asked for his work to be destroyed. All of his stories, his unfinished novels, were to be destroyed. I am sure there are some out there who were forced to read his work in school who wished that it did happen. But the man who was supposed to destroy the work upon Kafka's death, Max Brod, didn't. We are allowed to experience the work because of a bad friend breaking his word. Thank god.

A few years back a woman won a Banksy painting at an auction at Sotheby's. She paid 1.4 million dollars for the painting, Girl with Balloon. As soon as she won it and purchased it, Banksy's people activated a device in the painting's frame and the painting went down into the frame and was shredded. It was a prank to protest the moneyed world of art. I guess.

Don't think of it as a destruction of art but a transformation. The buyer kept the remains of the frame and the painting. Banksy renamed it as Love is in the Bin.

I know of many people who loved what Banksy did, but I am not too keen on the stunt. Because money still passed hands. He still got over a million dollars for the art. And the painting that the customer bid on and won, was destroyed. What was intended to be given for money was not.

I like the idea of destroying the art you make. I like the transitory. The ephemerol. It's when money is involved that it gets muddy and unpleasant.

The purest version of this, in my opinion, was by a local poet Tony Brown. Around twenty years ago he had a feature at the Java Hut. But he prepared for it differently than other poetry features he did.

He wrote brand new poems for the feature. He wrote them on the computer, printed them out, and then deleted the computer file. So the only copy of the poem was the print out. He did that for all these poems.

When he began, he asked for a volunteer. The way it then worked was that Tony read the poem and when it was one, it was given to the volunteer. The volunteer then had to tear it up into pieces. The poem is read, and then all evidence of the poem is destroyed.

I wasn't there. I missed it. Actually, Tony has done this type of feature a few more times and I missed each one. That first one is pretty legendary. People still talk of it. I heard the volunteer who had to rip up the pages was upset. Someone else built a little plexiglass container of the ripped up pages. I know of other poets have performed this way as well.

The poetry is just for that one moment. It is read and it cannot be read again. You might remember a line that was amazing, but after a while, you might remember it wrong. The poem changes in memory.

The art is not disposable. The way the poem makes you feel and think is not disposable. But it is created to not last.

I like this so much more than what Banksy did, because this didn't have a million dollar price tag to it.

This was about one instance where an artist shared with an audience for that one specific moment in time. Who says art needs to hang around? Who needs it more than once? If the work is good, powerful and true, it only needs one time to change a person.

Ten: Cardboard Records

You know I am so much cooler than all these hipsters who have discovered old records like they made them themselves. And how they all talk about vinyl. "I'm into vinyl." Or "The Music sounds truer when it's on vinyl."

Me? I don't go for that kind of record. Who needs something so common as vinyl? Me, I go for cardboard records.

What are cardboard records, I hear you cry? They are exactly what it sounds like. They were pieces of cardboard you played on your record player. They were coated with a thin plastic that had the grooves needed to make the music.

They sounded like shit. How could they not, they were made of cardboard. They came in magazines. They came as a premium at McDonald's. But for me, they came on the back of a cereal box.

On the back of specially marked boxes of Rice Krispies, there would be a section that you could cut out and like that, you have a cardboard record. And not just any record, but cardboard records with songs by everyone's favorite rock sensation, the Archies.

Oh, I guess I now have to explain the disposable art of the Archies. The Archies was a band with many hits like Sugary Sugar. Actually, the Archies were never a band. They were session musicians who threw together a bunch of bubblegum pop songs that played on the Archie cartoon show on Saturday Mornings. Archie and his band would play a song at the end of the cartoon and we would hear one of these songs made for the show.

There was a weird tradition in the cartoons of the sixties and seventies, that there should be new rocking music for the cartoons. It is an amazing concept, "Let's make disposable music for the disposable Saturday morning cartoon." It's like a puzzle box with wheels upon wheels.

The weird thing is, even though the Archies songs were never meant to be anything other than something in a cartoon, it made it to the radio. They played on America's Top Forty. Their songs were huge. I love the fakeness of the Archies. Who needs autotune when you have the cartoon redhead having a top ten hit.

But they were not the only band that had cardboard record success. On the back of Alphabits and Super Sugar Crisp cereals, you could get one of five Jackson Five records. The Jackson Five were huge, they were live people who became Saturday morning cartoons.

The amazing aspect to the whole cardboard record was that you had to cut it from the cereal box yourself. You had to cut out your own entertainment. You had to free it. Cut that out yourself. Kids these days, now you download all the music you want on your phone in just a few seconds while in my day, we had to cut our music our of the back of a Rice Krispies cereal box.

I remember cutting a few of these from the box and it was there that my deficit of cutting was evident. I have a memory of cutting one of the records too closely. I cut out the first thirty seconds of the song. Knowing the songs they used, I don't think I missed anything. But that does stress the fact that every cardboard record is a unique, one-of-a-kind objects d'art. Made from little hands, you can see the jagged cut lines represent man's struggle against nature.

Those records, which were on many a cereal box, did not last. Why didn't it survive? Well they were made of cardboard. They were not made to last. And they were given to kids and kids can never hold onto anything. And a lot of people got rid of all their records when that new thing the CD player came along and told us that any older technology is useless. Why would they hold onto something made of cardboard that played only two minutes of song when you weren't keeping all those full LPs?

It is the perfect piece of disposable art. They were cut, played once and then forgotten.

But I can't help but think of the kid who was raised with very little. She had nothing much of her own. I see her visiting her aunt and having a bowl of Rice Krispies and the aunt letting her cut out the record from the back of the box. There she is, walking home proudly, with the first music record that is hers and hers alone. I can see her playing that Archies record on her father's beat up record player until there is no more music left on the flimsy disc. The music is in her. Her first record. Her first song that was hers and hers alone.

When I see these pieces of cut up cardboard, I must think of the one who found it precious.

Update: *We got some reader response to this one. The writer remembered his favorite record, which was a flexi-disc that was included in an issue of Mad Magazine. The song was "She Got a Nose Job." I found it on YouTube and listened to it. And I am here to say, I survived. It was a tough go. Now, the funny part is that, if I was a kid, I would have thought this was the funniest damned thing I ever heard.*

Eleven: Autographed Copies

The recent passing of David Prowse, the actor who played Darth Vader in the first three Star Wars films, made me remember the one time I met him.

I was ten years old. It was 1979. I was visiting family in New York City. My Uncle, realizing that I loved comic books to an insane degree, took me to a new kind of store. It was a comic book shop. Who knew that such delights were even legal?

The shop was situated in the Upper East Side. It had the odd luck of being named Super Snipe. They took the name from an obscure 1940s comic book. Of course, when you looked at it, most comics were obscure

The shop was really small. You had to wait outside for others to leave. It could only fit ten customers at a time. When we did get in, I was in some higher plane of existence. A store dedicated to nothing but comic books. It was sublime.

It took me a few minutes to focus enough to see comics that I wanted. There was the first issue of the new series of Man-Thing. It was about a sentient swamp monster and I had to have it. I clutched it to my chest, afraid that someone would take it from me.

Suddenly, the door to the store opened and a giant strode in. It was amazing he could fit in the shop. A much smaller man ran like a terrier behind him and shouted, "David Prowse, Darth Vader himself is here and he will sign your Star Wars comics."

The giant of a man spoke to someone thrusting a comic at him. He had a lilting Scottish accent. I was bewildered, I saw Star Wars ten times, and that was not Darth Vader's voice. My uncle explained that David Prowse was in the costume and another actor, James Earl Jones, was the voice. I was dubious, but I had to give my uncle the benefit of the doubt. He had, afterall, taken me to a comic shop.

There was little room to avoid this huge celebrity. Soon, I was before him. He was six foot six. I was four foot something. I only came up to his abdomen. He was like a fairy tale creature. In that sweet, tenor voice he said to me, "You want me to sign your comic?"

Sure. I thrust in front of him my copy of Man-Thing #1. He opened it up and began to sign his name. He only made it to the letter "D" before his handler angrily said, "He's not going to sign that comic. Buy a Star Wars comic, he'll sign that." David Prowse nodded sadly from way up in the stratosphere.

Someone put into my hands a copy of Star Wars #29. It had a great cover of Darth Vader fighting a cyborg. Mr. Prowse took it and signed the first page. I believe he wrote, "David Prowse is Darth Vader."

He gave it back to me and now I had a comic I really didn't want, but it was signed by Darth Vader, so that must have been good. After only a few minutes, Darth Vader and his handler had left the building and we all were able to breathe again.

I love recalling that moment with David Prowse. This was before celebrities such as he would make a lot of money signing things. All I had to do was buy a forty cent Star Wars comic. Maybe that was the real worth of someone's signature back then.

Signatures are big time collectables. But all they are, are a name. An affirmation of identity. We force the value on it. We make it significant by sheer will.

Over the years, my comic book collection got to be immense. I sold it off a long time ago and I no longer have that signed Star Wars comic.

But the comic I probably miss more is that Man-Thing #1 with the letter "D" sprawled on the first page. Somewhere in the world, someone owns that copy of the book and am sure is annoyed that a crazy kid wrote on the first page, destroying the value. They don't know who graffitied on their book. Would they be impressed that Darth Vader wrote that letter "D"? Or would they still want it to be pristine and unblemished?

Update: *My sister wanted to remind me that she was also at Super Snipe that day and also met the giant that was David Prowse. I have no idea how I could ever have omitted my sister's existence when telling a cool story. How could I do such a thing?*

Twelve: Candy Necklace

I'm sure this happens to you all the time. You are sitting around, doing nothing, making no mischief, when a notion pops into your head, "What is the history of the candy necklace? And why are people not wearing them around to put a little sweetness into their bling?" Yes. We all have such thoughts, there is nothing to be ashamed to think such things.

Has anyone spent time, I mean serious time, wearing a candy necklace or the smaller, candy bracelet? Have you sashayed your way home with a few ounces of candy wrapped around your neck?

My son tells me of a kid at his school who would start the day with five candy bracelets on his wrist. He ate about a bracelet an hour. At the end of the day, he would be without candy bracelets and he also then spoke in a tongue that no one could understand.

No one knows the real origin of the candy bracelet. Some things of greatness are shrouded in mystery. One place said there was a rumor that they came from Northern Europe. I love the word they used, rumor. Like people, at candy conferences, whisper what their grandparents told them about a world in the frozen North where not only did people eat candy, but they wore it too.

What we do know for certain is that in the late fifties the candy necklace was introduced. They tend to use the Smarties candy.

I have to ask, who thought that candy worn around a kid's neck was a good idea? A kid who has been running around the neighborhood this entire humid day. And now that he needs a break, he will eat pieces of his necklace, for energy. There is nothing more delicious than a candy coated in neck sweat. Yum-yum.

I suppose it is either a candy dirty from sweat or the candy left alone on the kid's pocket, gathering up all the lint and tissue paper it can around its body. Wow. It just occurred to me. I am shocked about what our parents let us eat as kids.

The problem with candy necklaces as disposable art is that it really is not that artistic. It's just a string of sucking candies around a child's neck. It does not cry out, "This is art that was not meant to last!" The only thing it says to me when I see one around a fifth grader is, "Oh man, that kid is gonna be off the wall all afternoon!"

I am disappointed to not find any beautiful diamond rings made from the finest of hard candies. I guess they are out there, but I can't find them.

What I have found is candy turning into jewelry, not the other way around. There are a few jewelers who take candy and encase it in resin. They then put the resined candy on necklaces or earrings or rings. You want licorice candy earrings or a Jordan almond necklace? That can happen. With real candy, but you can't eat it. It will last for years. It can be a heirloom handed down from daughter to daughter. "I am giving you your grandmother's favorite piece of jewelry, the tennis bracelet made from gummy bears. I know she will be smiling down when you wear it."

This would not fit as disposable art. This is art that uses candy as a starting block. I pity the candy starved fool who tries to bite into the Jordan Almond ring.

I guess what I would like to see is someone wearing a candy necklace and not eating it away until it is only naked elastic. They could eat it, they could make it go away, but chose not to. They like the way it looks on them. They like that pop of pastel color around their neck. They are not saving the dessert for later, but making a fashion statement for the here and now.

And when your friends see that you are no longer sporting such a fine piece of jewelry around your neck, you can tell them, "I needed a change of style. And besides, I got hungry."

Thirteen: Video Game Music

Sitting down in the office to write this, my son came to join in, writing his own things. He took out a record and put it on the stereo. It is the soundtrack to Battlefield V. It is a lush orchestral piece of music. It is sad and monumental, at turns. And it was written for a video game. My son has been introduced to so many different kinds of music because of video games. He found a love of 40s harmony groups, such as the Ink Spots, from playing Fallout. He discovered Willie Nelson through Red Dead Redemption 2. And the Battlefield games have a large cinemascope type soundtrack.

This should not be a big surprise. Video game music is a big thing. A lot of musicians make some living wages from putting out music for the latest first person shooter. Scott Campbell, the founder of Post Modern Jukebox, made his first splash by making music for a Biohazard game. Large philharmonic orchestras have their most financially successful concerts when they program video game music. How are people introduced to music now? Through the music they hear every day, shooting em up, rescuing the princess. That kind of thing.

I am old. To me the music of video games were the plink-plink-plink of the ball hitting the paddle on a game of Pong. Or the pwew-pwew shooting sounds in Galaga. The only way to hear such a melody was to put a quarter in the game and play your three lives. It was like listening to songs on a jukebox. I know, what the hell is a jukebox?

For me, the most iconic music from video games has to be from Super Mario Brothers. And the amazing thing about that music, is that the composer, Koji Kondo was quite limited by the amount of space he had for the pre-recorded sound. He could not go crazy with what he could do. So with such limitations, comes a melody we all know and love. Do we love it because of the ingenuity or in spite of it?

If you want to go down a rabbit hole, or a drain pipe because we are talking about Mario Brothers, then go to YouTube and put in a Super Mario Brothers theme cover. There are a lot of choices. My favorite at the moment is the Post Modern Jukebox (them again) where they do it with a Dixey Land combo and a tap dancer. Got to have a tap dancer for your video game music covers!

There are books that analyze the music from that first Super Mario Brothers book. The books explain that the music is there to create a mood. It allows you to know what is coming. If the music speeds up, then you better speed the hell up too, because you are running out of time to clear that world. Different music tells you that there are new expectations.

The music was there to inform the player about certain things. And also, it needed to swing baby!

Kondo, who has done tons of great music for games, has been interviewed endlessly about the original Super Mario Brothers music. In one of the interviews, he said, "music is inspired by the game controls, and its purpose is to heighten the feeling of how the game controls." I love that. The music was a teaching tool to start to understand how to play the game better. It was not meant to be covered by countless performers on YouTube. Its purpose was to help you get to the Princess with efficiency. To win the game. To save the day.

A few years ago, we took the kid to FunSpot in Laconia, New Hampshire. It has something like 300 vintage video games. That's a lot of sound. That's a lot of 8 Bit Music playing at once. When we walked in, it was like the sound of all that composition playing at once would knock us over. It was a riot of music and sound designed to entice you to play this one and not that one. It was there to help you learn when to jump, when to shoot, when to run away fast. There was no way to hear any one game. It was a whirlwind of sampling and explosions. The only way to hear one song was to lean into your chosen game and get as close to the action as possible. You had to give yourself up to the game to hear the song. A song of play and conflict and rebirth (usually three lives per quarter.) An earworm. You will be singing that tiny tinny melody for the rest of the day. Or even longer.

Update: *The book I stole most of my information from was from the Bloomsbury Series: 33 ⅓. It is a wonderful series and I can't recommend it too highly. This one was "Koji Kondo's Super Mario Bros Soundtrack" by Andrew Schwartmann.*

Fourteen: Decorative Hand Soap

Okay. Soap that you are not allowed to use. It was a thing. Most of the time, they were in the shape of a shell. They were in the bathroom. They were probably below a nicely folded hand towel, that you were also not supposed to touch.

In most tellings of this, it's the grandmother who has the bowl of decorative soap. And do not piss off grandma. I wouldn't even look at those soaps. You have been warned.

I have a lot of questions about this. The first being, why should there be soap that is not allowed to be used? It's soap! The very definition of the thing means that you touch it. In this new age of social distancing and constant handwashing, we see a piece of soap, we expect to use it. But you put it in the form of a shell and it's a huge, do not enter sign flashing.

The next question I have is, why seashells? It's almost always soap in the shape of the discarded hard outer layer of a sea creature. The real shells are created by the animals. The soap shells were made from a mold in a factory. What makes the facsimile of a seashell such an important artifact?

My last question has to be, why did all the grandmothers protect these pieces of cleaning material like they were masterpieces on loan from the Louvre?

To see if I might get some answers to these questions, I put them all to the Board of Directors of the Library of Disposable Art (a venerable crowd). They responded that they too had experience with the Verboten Soap!

Jeff Campbell tells us, "My mom had these translucent bars... they had like shells or stones or something in them? She was this incredibly kind, loving and compassionate woman. And she utterly lost her shit when my young cousin clawed them, used them to wash his hands." Paul McMahon clarifies what types of soap he was dealing with, "

Mostly shaped like scallop shells and shark eye shells. Maybe even a starfish one."

Christine Guest tells an almost optimistic tale, "My grandma had a pair that looked like cameos. One had Martha Washington's face, the other George. I think they were bi-centenial things? I did wash my hands with Martha, but Grandma was gracious about it." A gracious grandma dealing with matters of the decorative soap? Not in my neighborhood!

The part I really don't get is that even though we are not allowed to use the soap, it is always placed right there in the bathroom, inches from the sink. It's like it is mocking us.

The always philosophical Deb Middleton was able to shine some light when she wrote, " It was something you just had to have to have the proper, respectable home. It was also a status symbol, you had enough money to have something decorative like that, even if you didn't, it made people think you did." Well, that definitely answers some of the questions. It was an affordable way to look classy. And if it is losing definition because the soap is being used, then it ain't classy no more.

The other name I came across for this item was Guest Soap. This was the good soap for the good people who might visit. The kids are not good. Let them use ugly, ordinary soap. The kind of soap we are ashamed of.

Decorative soap is a perfect candidate for the Library of Disposable Art. If the soap is used correctly, then it should be worn down to nothing. It should keep your hands clean, not be pleasing to the eye and nose (because a lot of these little darlings were scented). Soap, in whatever shape it may be in, is meant to lather and shrink. Soap is a functional tool. It should not be encased in plastic, like the furniture in your aunt's front room.

There are still mysteries to this phenomena. Mostly, why shells? Really. Why is the motif always seashells? Stuff like that keeps me up at night.

But this is an issue that seems to be fading. All the people who responded to my queries are middle aged. We are remembering our grandmothers doing this. But what of our children? They probably were not exposed to such prohibitions, because we wouldn't do it to them. We let our kids use the soap, because dammit, it's soap. We will not subject them to this because we still have the scars. It makes us feel all dirty. Like we need to wash up. With whatever piece of soap is at hand.

FIfteen: Collectible Glasses

The other day, I noticed one of our Star Wars glasses sitting on the coffee table, minding its own business, I am sure. I picked it up and brought it over to the sink. I placed it down in the sink, with a vague plan of washing it sometime that evening. I didn't get the chance. The act of placing it in the sink caused it to lose its will to be whole. It broke into five large pieces. I slowly fished them out and threw them away.

Now you should know, they aren't just any Star Wars glasses you can pick up at Target. No, sir. Not for us. No, we are too cool for Target pop culture detritus. No, these were vintage glasses given as a promotion for the Return of the Jedi. They are from a long time ago, 1983. That makes them 37 years old. They were given out with an order of Coke at Burger King.

There were five or six different Return of the Jedi glasses, collect them all if you dare. They have wrap around illustrations of scenes from the movie. There are Ewoks and C3PO. There is the glass about Han Solo on the Moon of Endor. And there is the one with Jabba the Hutt on the Sand Barge. (For those of you not Star Wars fans, you are reading this wondering what off market drugs I might be taking, but be reassured, that all of this makes serious sense, for those in the know) It was a premium. If you bought a certain type of drink, you got the glass. You might have to pay a little more for the glass, but why wouldn't you? You are getting a delicious Whopper and a great Star Wars glass. You should buy extra. Who knows. They might be valuable years from now.

I think I bought one of these glasses for the first time at That's Entertainment, the great comic and weirdness shop in the city. My son, who was eight at the time, thought it was the greatest thing in the world. He felt that chocolate milk tasted better in the glass. Who am I to disagree with such a reasoned opinion?

But it was made of glass. Glass feels good when you drink from it. Glass also breaks. It wasn't too long before we had no Star Wars:

Empire Strikes Back Burger King Glass. My son was upset. He was in tears.

Father to the rescue. I went on EBay and bought a set of six of the glasses. They came two weeks later with two of the glasses broken. So we had four.

This has been the history of these glasses. We buy them on EBay and one by one they shatter into history. This is how it has gone for years.

So, the other day one of the glasses of the latest set broke and I told my son and reminded him that we had two left. He was upset. I wasn't expecting it. He is twelve now and I figured maybe there wouldn't be such an attachment to 40 year old fast food restaurant premiums."I like having them. My favorite ones always break first." Father to the rescue.

And over the years, the damned glasses are getting more expensive on EBay. This stands to reason because as the years pass we all break these things and they become slightly more scarce. There are still a lot of them out there, but gone are the days I could get a full set for twelve bucks.

I like them. I drink from an Ewoks glass or a Jabba the Hutt glass almost every day. My son does not. These are not the glasses he is looking for. He likes looking at them. He likes our act of possession. But he just would rather drink from a wider glass.

Soon, we will break so many of them that they will become too valuable to drink from. They will have to be kept away from the vagaries of finger muscles and stress fractures. They will be kept in a cabinet used solely for their safety. They will be kept under glass.

And to think, these were pieces of promotion. They said "Collect Them All" and wanted you to buy them. No one expected them to change into something worthy. They would do things that would be kept and preserved and cried over when all that remains are shards.

Update: *Just yesterday, I was cleaning the last Star Wars glass we had and the damned thing cracked. I tossed. That's it. The end. The question I have not answered is if I should get another batch from online sellers. It is getting pricier and pricier. Oh, the dilemmas we have.*

Sixteen: The Pet's in the Mail

When I was a kid, I think one of the best parts about the comics I picked up at the drug store were the ads. I was fascinated about the full page ads for the Sea Monkees. I never bought them, because I didn't want my mail order animals to have human-like faces. If I was to judge from what I would get from the picture, I was going to get small human-like creatures, and I just didn't think I could handle that.

There were also all the ads to teach me how to be big and muscled. I was no longer going to have sand kicked in my face, even if I was cool about it. Or I could not just be buff, but have the martial arts skills to kill a man with a viper technique. This sounded like a good investment of my five dollars.

Recently, I have dived back into these old mags and I linger on these weird little ads. There was one that made me pause. It was a small one, only a few inches in size, but gigantic in imagination.

It read. "Baby Raccoons! One of America's Favorite Pets! Has always been and still is. Easy to care for. $29.95 with cage. Send cashier's check or money order along with your phone number and nearest airport. Hialeah Pets. Department 35. Hialeah, Florida."

America's favorite pet? Really? In what America? And the idea that these are baby raccoons and not full grown ones. As if they will never grow up. They are Peter Pan raccoons. The lost boys of scavenger animals. And don't you think your mother will be so excited for you to have a pet at last?

In my house growing up, we were not allowed pets. We could have hamsters and gerbils, but they hardly count as pets. They are more ornaments with wood chips.

The part that gets me the most is that there are at least 34 other departments at this most reputable of mail order pet purveyors. From another ad I saw online, there is a department 16 where the monkeys are purchased. I wonder what other impractical pets are behind the other numbers. What a joy. What a natural disaster.

I was able to find online a story by a guy who claims that he saved his money and ordered a monkey from one of these ads. He was able to get someone to pick it up at the airport. And when he got the monkey out of the cage, it immediately tore the kid's face up. Can you blame it? The family kept the monkey, but it did not live long.

For me, I think these ads are important not for getting a wild animal through the mail, but just to imagine what joy it would be to own a monkey or a baby raccoon. The price was high for a kid back then, so all we could do was dream. "All the kids will see me with my monkey on a leash and think I am so cool."

The quality of the daydream is up to how much you can believe. The ads in the old comics were fantasy. Things we can create in our heads. What a joy. What a natural disaster.

Seventeen: Scented Candles

When I was a young man, I lived in Hyannis in Cape Cod. We got an apartment close to downtown, which was great. The rent was cheap. Probably because it was two miles from the Cape Cod airport and planes were constantly flying overhead. And another reason is that we were a block away from the Colonial Candle Factory. At all hours of the day, a toxic cloud of mixed votive scents invaded the neighborhood. If we were stumbling home after a night of sampling the Hyannis bars, we were immediately sobered up through the boot camp version of aromatherapy that was passing the candle factory. All traces of alcohol fled from the one two combo punch of vanilla and patchouli. We would inhale when we reached the block and exhaled only after passing the factory.

That might be why I just don't understand the scented candle scene. Some of the candles smell nice, but then you have to remember to burn them safely. And sometimes what smelled nice in the store now feels like it's stinking up your home. For some people, they love using the scented candles. For others, they just don't understand why they were given it as a present by a distant cousin. Do I look like a candle person?

My wife gave me a Father's Day gift of a candle that had the scent of pipe smoke. Now, I don't smoke. But I have admitted to my wife that one of my fondest memories of my father is the pipe always dangling out of his mouth, and the persistent odor of the sweet tobacco wherever he had been. That's a fine present. I am happy I got it. Now, I don't ever plan to light it, because we don't use candles in the house. And even though the odor brings back many memories, do I want the house smelling of it? Nostalgia is a wonderful thing, but do you want the house stinking of it?

A few years ago, a company put out a five candle mini-votive set in honor of Star Wars: A New Hope. Each candle had a different and distinct odor. You had five iconic aspects of the film masterpiece enshrined in scent. There was: Bantha Milk, Wookie, X-Wing Cockpit, Trash Compactor and Canteen. Those are some all over the place scents. A review commented that none of the scents were awful, but none were particularly pleasing either. Say what you will about a candle set that has Trash Compactor as a scent, the set sold out quickly.

But the question I have for those that bought for it themselves or for their dear friends, did anyone plan on using them as candles? This was something witty and fun to show to friends when they came over. They will ask, "Have you used them?" and you will reply, "Are you crazy?" A conversation starter more than anything else. That set has value because no one would ever use it for its intended purpose.

Candles are an odd creature. It makes light. The flame itself is beautiful, you can be lost in the flicker and fade that you stare at in the center of the flame. The candle also can be gorgeously constructed. They are pieces of sculpture art and there are many candles that will never be burned. They are just pretty as is. Like the decorative soaps and the fancy hand towels that grandma insists never to be used, there is a breed of candle that is lit at your own risk.

Scented candles are slightly different. They usually are not pretty looking. They are supposed to smell pretty, or soothing. Some people use them. Some people keep them in their bathroom closet, because his sister in-law insists on giving them as gifts. Is she trying to say the house stinks?

But even if you use five scents at once and the place smells confused, the odor will pass. It will not last. Like the candle burning at both ends, it doesn't stick around. Like all things of disposable art, it stays on as a memory. Hey, you remember when the apartment smelled of rose hips? Or, the fact that that smell of pipe brings my father back for a brief second, like a quick flicker of a candle flame?

Eighteen: Toys in the Box

One of the first fights my wife and I ever had was when she moved in with me and we unpacked her Charlie Brown toy figures. She had a lot of them. Snoopy and Woodstock. There was Lucy and Linus dressed for Halloween. (I got a rock.) The little action figures were still in the original packaging. "Why don't you take them out so you can pose them and play with them?" She gave me a steely look and I had the sensation that I said something VERY bad. She informed me that taking them out of the package was a deal break for the relationship. They came in the original packaging and they were going to stay that way.

But this is not about me. This is about the refusal of many adults to take their toys out of the package. There is a whole generation of toy creatures that will be forever encased in original plastic.

You know what is better than having a Boba Fett action figure? Having a Boba Fett action figure that has never been taken out of the package. Or a Donatello Ninja Turtle doll. That thing better be in its plastic card for it to be worthy of collecting.

This has been a thing for decades with toy collectors. Toys in the original box are better than the toys themselves. We want things to be pristine. We want things to be untouched by human hands.

But the things that are untouched by human hands, were meant to be played with by kids. I know we are adults and are wrapped with mortality and nostalgia. We want the toys of our youth. We begin to collect Star Wars or Ninja Turtles or Transformers. And to really make it perfect. Not only do we plan to never play with the toy we spent so much money on, we demand that no one else ever touched it as well. We want our toys to be like cloistered nuns.

What you will have is a piece of plastic encased in plastic. You will have an object d'art and not a toy. You will have a facsimile of a toy.

I know that I am annoying all the toy collectors out there, but I will say it. Screw the resale value. Take the toys out and have some fun. You know, fun. Like playing with the toys you loved when you were a kid.

Display your GI Joe toys in odd poses. Let them cavort with the Barbie dolls that you also released from their plastic prison. Put them in dioramas. Perch them on the edge of bookshelves. Take them out in the wild and take action photographs with them. Hold on to that doll you always wanted when you were a kid, and whisper small truths into its plastic ear.

That Meco Spider Man action figure from 1975 is dying in his box. He can't breathe. He is suffocating. He has been stuck in that box for 46 years. Imprisoned with no trial. No crime. He is the victim of the insidious penal system and the toy market. Release him now. The DNA evidence has come back inconclusive. Free the Holly Hobby Seven!

I don't understand the appeal of a toy that has never been played with. It doesn't feel like a thing of great value. It feels like the saddest creation in the world.

Nineteen: Miniature Liquor Bottles

Last time I was in Vermont, I went into a junk shop. Here is a question, when did we stop calling stores with an accumulation of stuff, junk shops? Now they are antique malls. Or vintage emporiums. When did we stop calling them junk shops? Now, I am not denigrating the things found in such places. I mean, some of my best friends are junk.

Whatever you need to call it, this place was a packed and over teeming cornucopia of junk, and I loved it. I was wandering about, with no intention to buy anything. My wife really is done with me buying useless things to clutter the house with. She says, I clutter the house well enough just by my very presence. No need to bring anything else into the mix.

But then, near the register, there was a large box that said, "Old bottles. One dollar each." These were not just old bottles. They were miniature old bottles. They were miniature old liquor bottles.

You know. Nips. Those shrunken vessels found in hotel mini-bars and in the rolling beverage carts of airplanes. Or you might find them stuffed inside a pinata. (This is true. A friend told me that for her partner's 30th birthday, they had a pinata filled with nips. Though that was not a great idea what with them being hit with a bat and then falling on the ground, they did tend to break all over the place.)

I rummaged through the box and found the three most interesting shaped bottles. The guy at the counter was amused I was buying them. "You know, some of them still have some of their booze in them." As if this was an enticing selling point.

I just smiled at him and handed over my three bucks. I couldn't explain to him that these three old bottles were wonderful examples of disposable art. Nothing is more disposable than a nip bottle. They are not meant to hang about. They are to be carried in a pocket and quickly consumed and then tossed away.

Next time you walk through the neighborhood, look down at the gutter and you will see nips tossed here, there and the next place. Conceptual art of the quick buzz. The stratification of thirst shrunk down to its smallest dividend.

I can't conceive of anyone keeping these bottles. Each one is at least twenty five years old. Why would anyone keep them? But someone did. Looking on eBay, I found that some of these bottles are for sale for over ten dollars. No one is saying that the seller will get such a fortune, but they are trying.

They are dirty things, this trio. In the bottle of Guest House Port Wine there is a dark purple crust on the bottom from the dried wine. The Sabra Chocolate Orange Liquor bottle (a fine Isreali product, that is now no longer made in Israel) also has the dried remnants of its elixir caked on the inside of the bottle. Someone didn't drink every drop.

It is impossible to clean them. If you wash them out, you will ruin the paper label. So you are stuck with a dusty old bottle with a few drops of bad port wine. (That friend who had the Nip Pinata was shocked that I was not going to taste the few remaining drops of port wine. She felt I was a poor columnist for not tasting what I am writing about. Well, anyone who has ever read this column knows what a poor columnist I am, so why ruin my taste buds?)

I bought the last ancient nip bottle for its name. Camus Cognac. I do love a bottle of booze named after 20th Century French Existentialists. If you need to understand the Myth of Sissyphus, just have a few sips of this, and it will all make sense.

We are pack rats. We keep everything. We even keep the glass that held the booze we drank too quickly the night before. Hangovers are transitory. The glass that gave us that pain can stay with us as long as we have shelf space.

I picked the bottles because they were a nice shape. According to my research, the Sabra bottle is based on an ancient Phoenecian decanter. See. Fancy. The Guest House Port Wine is three sided. Two of the sides have indentations, probably to aide in tipping that bad boy back and having the drink slide right down the throat.

My wife saw them and mused that they looked like perfume bottles. I am sure there were many people given scent from these bottles.

Looking at them on a shelf, what joy of art will you find? What absence will you feel?

Update: *I still have these three little bottles on my work desk in the home office. Why? Why do I keep them? I did the writing and I don't think they are that charming. But there is a fear of getting rid of things that I wrote about. Maybe I will want to write more. Maybe I just like physical trophies of the things I wrote. Or maybe I should just dump them in the gutter like all the other nips and broken dreams we have clogging up our pockets.*

Twenty: Tea Box Menagerie

I don't know why I was ignorant about these critters, but I had no idea about the Red Rose Tea Figurines. My family drank Lipton Tea. We were not Red Rose folk. When I asked some people in the Library Braintrust what I should write about next, several of them mentioned the Red Rose Animals.

Red Rose Animals?

I asked my wife about them. "Did you know that there are little animals in the boxes of tea? I guess it's a thing."

My wife gave me one of those exasperated, husbands are the dumbest creatures looks, stared at my sorry face and said, "We have them all over the house. My grandma loved them. I keep them for her. I mean I have some right there." She pointed to a bookcase, and right on top was a tiny ceramic polar bear. There was a bison. There was a capuchin monkey. (Actually, I have no idea if it is a capuchin monkey, but I am feeling kind of dumb right now, so I figured being specific about what type of monkey will improve my standing.)

On another bookcase, I was greeted with a proud, but wee, lion. "How did I not know that these figures were here?"

My wife sighed audibly and left for the downstairs, where there were, no doubt, more Red Rose beasties waiting upon her entrance.

My house is a preserve of tiny figurine creatures. I live amongst the wild beasts. I just wish I knew about it. I am curious what other things I haven't noticed. Husbands are stupid.

But I am a writer of disposable art, so I did my research. Thank you Internet!

The little figures are called Wade Whimsies. They started hanging out in boxes of Red Rose Tea in 1967 in Canada. We in America were not graced with such joy until 1983. There are not just animals. You might be blessed with a popular landmark in tiny glory.

There are some that are just weird like one of the heads from Easter Island. A polar bear in your tea is charming and worth keeping. An ancient totem from a Pacific Island? Yeah. That's a tosser.

My wife has them because they remind her of her grandmother. She bought them at thrift stores and antique marts for a couple bucks each. This is an affordable way to keep memories alive. We are always trying to bring back those who are missing. If you can do that with a wee snow leopard that you got for less than a king sized candy bar, then you are living your best life.

But most people who have them got them from the Red Rose Tea box. I don't know if people bought the tea just for the figures, but it's a nice thing to find in a box of something you were going to have anyway. I like tea. I like small ceramic figurines. There is nothing wrong with getting something for nothing.

And that something is easy to place on a shelf. They are so small and unobtrusive. You can be like me, living with them for years unaware. I lived with animals? I did? But that is the joy of little things. Now I am aware of them. Now I walk around the house and see the things I didn't know were there. The other life forms. Maybe I will be more aware of things in general. Maybe I will not trip over my winter boots. Maybe I will finally find those spare keys I have been looking for.No doubt, the little yorkie figurine took them and hid them away in his miniature lair. Maybe that's where all the socks went too. Blame the Wade Whimsies. They are everywhere.

Twenty-One: Old Receipts (Left on the Curb)

Last Monday, I was heading into Nick's for the Monday Trivia when I saw Jeff picking up pieces of paper from the gutter of the street. Jeff is one of the regulars at Monday Trivia and I was not expecting him to be picking trash on such a lovely evening.

"Trash collector, your new vocation?" I asked.

Jeff looked up and gave me a smile of welcome. "Dave, there are all of these papers. They are old."

"Yeah, trash usually isn't new and shiny. Trash is mostly old. Mostly."

Jeff looked at me a little confused and then said, "Sure. But all of these papers are really old. Look," he said, holding up several pieces of paper. "These two are both dated 1970. That's pretty old."

I finally gazed at the curb and there were a few small piles of papers nestled by the tire of a car that just happened to be there. I leaned down and plucked up an invoice. I read it out to Jeff. It was a bill from Morse Brothers Electrical Company. The invoice date was January 20, 1970. It was sent to an insurance agency on Millbury Street. The insurance agency has been out of business for ages, though the sign still looms over the street.

We were joined by Mr. Dan who got into the swing of things and found some invoices of his own on the street. I read from the 51 year old invoice like it was some broken catechism. "In the work performed section they had typed Wire new lavatory. Install plugs. Wire commercial rate 20 gallon water heater. Wire meter trough and 60 amp MR switch."

We all got two or three letters and invoices in that little corner of Millbury Street. They were all dated 1970. I had a receipt of payment to Abbott Animal Hospital. It was marked paid 3/14/70. I wasn't aware of it, but Jeff and Mr. Dan informed me that Abbott was still in business. I wondered if they wanted their paperwork back. It was a little bit out of date, but it was still theirs.

What an odd site on Millbury Street. Three grown men picking up yellowed old pieces of paper from the dirty street and celebrating each scrap like it was a lost treasure. Like it told something important. I am sure the smart people of the neighborhood ignored we three maniacs.

Without saying it, we all picked a few of the old papers and kept them. We planned to hold on to them. We don't know why.

When we got into the bar, Sean the Bartender, rolled his eyes at us and asked, "What were you three knuckleheads doing dumpster diving in the middle of the street?"

We told him of our great discovery. We showed him the papers we now hoarded to us like Smiegel and his precious ring. He reiterated that we were idiots. We agreed. He then told us that he saw someone cleaning out the insurance agency office earlier in the day. The guy was carrying boxes of old papers out into a van.

It now made sense to us. This wasn't a strange wormhole we fell through. This was some papers from the 1970 box of receipts falling out onto the street when they were being loaded up. Well, maybe this is a kind of temporal wormhole.

These papers are worthless things. 51 years old. It tells of money owed, money paid. But I have found great joy in looking at them. I love how everything was typed out. All the itemized materials were painstakingly hunt and pecked through a typewriter. For the electrical invoice,we learned of the effort involved. They billed for ten and three quarters hours of labor. The electrician was worth nine dollars an hour. That's how much we pay for a licensed electrician now, right?

There is a story in these discarded pieces of commerce. Someone paid 22 dollars to have their animal looked at. Did it go well? Was it some daughter's beloved dog? Their cat? The receipt said the reference number for the transaction was 25,921. If we could look up the file, what stories might we discover?

For each of these invoices, these receipts, there are fragments of lives being lived. These invoices are tiny pinhole portals to gaze at half a century ago. But the holes are so small, we can barely see a thing. But that doesn't mean we shouldn't try to gaze back. To see the people who lived these receipts.

I am not advocating that we should gather up last week's CVS receipts and contemplate them like art on a museum wall. But let's not kid ourselves that these scraps of paper don't have stories to tell. They color in the blank areas of our collective memory. And they will be more pleasant clutter in my house, in my life.

And to any business looking for some old invoices, you can alway find Jeff, Mr. Dan or myself at Trivia most Mondays. We might have the old scraps you need.

Update: Sad to say, by the time you read this, you will not have a chance to go to Nick's. It's last day is April 4th, 2022. It was a great place to hangout with friends or to sneak into the back booths and write. Just another scrap to flutter in the wind.

Twenty-Two: Pine Cones

I was doing what I usually do, aimlessly wandering around a junk shop. I was just window shopping. Really, I am under strict orders from my wife to not bring home any junk shop stray I have absconded with. So I was just looking at all the lovely bits of refuse. And it appeared that I was also hearing the lovely refuse. I was hearing a conversation going on in a large wooden bowl. No one was around but me and all the junk. I leaned in close and saw that there were three pine cones in the bowl and they were having a heated conversation. I suppose all conversation between pine cones is always fiery. They didn't notice me, so I crouched down underneath the table made from a salvaged door and recorded their conversation on my phone.

First Pine Cone: Come on now, why do you think we are even in this bowl?

Second Pine Cone: Haven't I told you? Because it is decorative.

First Pine Cone: What do you mean, that we pine cones are decoration.

Second Pine Cone: You are twisting my words one more time. We are not decoration. We are part of an assemblage of disparate parts that are placed together, creating a heightened sense of pleasure for the design.

First Pine Cone: Three pine cones tossed in a fifty year old wooden bowl? That's a thing of the art of design? But they do. They place a bowl on table and put in pine cones. Who thought that was a good idea? And did anyone ask us if we wanted to participate in such a farce?

Second Pine Cone: We become the symbol of the connection to nature. They are never in a sterile home as long as there are some pieces of the forest in a bowl. We become the offering for a good, natural life.

First Pine Cone: And why us? Because we are cheap and plentiful. No one pays for a pine cone at a craft super store. You just go and pick them up from the ground. We are the road kill of the home decor world. And the homeowner feels good because they made something earthy and homespun and didn't have to spend any money at Pottery Barn.

Second Pine Cone: Can't we be beautiful both in nature and in a nice table display?

First Pine Cone: Nature. We are holders of seeds. We are made to propagate the pine tree, not to be pretty to look at it.

Third Pine Cone: I agree, we aren't things that should just be looked at and gazed upon. We have the chance to get out of this wooden bowl prison and make a difference with kids. We can work together and have the children learn so much.

First Pine Cone: Are you talking about pre-school crafts. I thought that they stopped doing that to us due to allergies.

Third Pine Cone: You mean the pine cone bird feeders? What a great activity. Have the children spread peanut butter on our appendages and then cover the peanut butter with bird seed. Hang us on a tree and then watch in amazement as the birds peck at us.

Second Pine Cone: That is so barbaric. We are smeared in peanut butter and set upon by birds? What nightmare world did we awaken in?

First Pine Cone: That nightmare world has a name. It is kindergarten. Hear that word and tremble in fear.

Second Pine Cone: But they don't use us that way. Not because they are concerned with us, but that peanut butter now causes distress in some children. We are saved due to the sudden influx of nut allergies.

Third Pine Cone: First off, there was nothing wrong with being a bird feeder. It's a useful act. And second, just because we are not that anymore doesn't mean that we are needed in the STEM based classroom.

First Pine Cone: What, are we STEM teachers now? Does that mean we are in the teacher's union?

Third Pine Cone: Don't be ridiculous. We are used in a variety of projects. Because we are cheap and easily found, we are used often. Don't think of it as being misused, but that our ubiquity has made us essential to the learning process.

First Pine Cone: And how have we done such a thing while stuck in a wooden bowl in a junk shop?

Third Pine Cone: There is so much fun that we can be part of. They can learn so much about nature through us. In one they put three pine cones, like us, in three jars. One is just air. One has the pine cone in cold water. The third has the pine cone in hot water. The kids get to observe what changes occur. And do you know what they see?

First Pine Cone: I don't care what they learn. How can you think about what the kids learn when two of our pine cone brethren are drowned in jars of water? That is so barbaric.

Third Pine Cone: Okay. So you don't like learning science. How about art? They can paint with us. They can paint us and glue us together to make a wreath. Or with pipe cleaners, we turn into a halloween spider. Or we can be an owl. It's amazing what transformation awaits us in the art area of a preschool class. I feel honored by all the attention.

Second Pine Cone: The attention of turning into something we never were meant to be? No thank you. Just put me in a bowl and let me be beautiful on my own.

First Pine Cone: Just leave me on the ground. Let me be part of the forest carpet. Like I was always meant to be.

Third Pine Cone: Where's the fun in that?

First Pine Cone: I won't be able to explain it to you if you just don't get it.

And realizing that the junk shop owner was looking at me sideways, I decided that I didn't get it either, and left without making a purchase.

Twenty Three: QSL Cards

Sometimes, when you enter the Library of Disposable Art, you can look at what's there and get it right away. "Hey, that's a T-Shirt." Or "Look at those cute ceramic animals that came from the tea box." You can understand what they are and figure out for yourself if it is cool or not. Then there are some alcoves in the library that have items that make a fella scratch their head in confusion. What the hell is this and why do people collect them?

And this is not me attacking the lovers of Hummel figurines (though I just don't get that one bit. Those are nightmare inducing totems.). No, this is not about your personal taste, but things that you look at and don't understand and when someone explains it to you, you still don't understand. It's like we are suffering from bric-a brac aphasia.

That is the case with QSL cards. I have a zine that reproduces authentic QSL cards from Washington State during the 1970s. You see. I wrote the words using as much English as I ever was taught, and yet the damn sentence does not make much sense. But just because it is odd for myself and you (probably) does not mean that somewhere in town, there are several people with large collections of these aforementioned QSL cards.

What are QSL cards? I'm glad you asked. Actually, I have been dreading this part of the column. The part where I explain what I am going on about. I have never been an ace at making myself clear (see earlier essays in the series to prove my point.) And I feel like I might not make much sense (so what else is new?). But here goes.

When people communicate to each other through Ham Radio or through CB radio, they will reach one person somewhere in the globe. That is the purpose. To contact another lover of Ham or CB. To reach somewhere you never have reached before.

When you do have contact with someone, the routine is to send a QSL card to a central processing center and they will then send the card to the other person involved in the conversation. The QSL card has the user's personal information on it. It will also give details of the contact the two users had. This card means, "I acknowledge this transmission." People collect these cards to show where all the people they spoke to over their radio were. They try to get cards delivered from as far as possible.

The cards themselves can be plain postcards with just the info printed on it. But in the peak of the CB craze in the 70s, the cards became illustrated. They had funny cartoons on them. They had pictures. There were people who made a living drawing QSL card cartoons. They are a little bit folk art, a little bit underground comix and a touch of "what the hell is this."

I was going through the zine that had all of these examples of QSL cards and an old friend confessed he was getting his Ham Radio license. He told me that he loves QSL cards. He still gets them. He is in the process of creating the image for his own card, which will be an aerial photo of his hometown.

This blew me away. The idea that people still do this is crazy to me. That they still use Ham radios to communicate with and use postcards to acknowledge that moment of contact with another. Yesterday, I spoke to a co-worker in Oaxaca, Mexico. I picked up my mobile phone and we chatted about work for a half hour. While it was sleeting here in New England, he described the 75 degree weather he was afforded outside his house in the mountains. Do we need Ham radio to shrink the world? Do we need kitschy postcards to say that, "I am here. And for a moment, we spoke together over a radio. Are we here together?"

And for some of us, the answer is yes. Yes. I need to talk to someone outside of Zoom and unlimited minutes. I need to put some effort in the act of reaching out. I need to get something in the mail, something that was touched by many hands, to say that we are all here together.

The world is a lot smaller than we ever thought it would be. But we need to put some effort into it. We need funny postcards sent to us, to remind us of the world that is all around us. We need someone to say to us, in the friendliest tone possible, "I acknowledge this transmission."

Update: *Just another thank you to one of my dearest and oldest friends. Foster really got me to understand the whole concept of the QSL card. If there is still confusion while reading, the fault is mine. He explained it to me with kindness and clarity. Foster told me he tried to get the aerial photo for QSL card, but it didn't turn out well, so he went for another image of his town.*

Twenty Four: Cell Animation

When I picked up my cell animation from Framed in Tatnuck, I gave my name and the woman said, "Oh you had the animated dragon."

For some ridiculous reason, I took offense at this. "No. That's not a dragon. That's Godzooki." The woman, a trained framing professional, looked at me like I was a crazy person.

I was worse than a crazy person, I was a collector of nostalgia. There is nothing more annoying. If you get something wrong about my collection, I will have to correct you in the snootiest way possible.

Let's stop here for a moment. There is a lot to unpack in the first hundred words of this column.

What is cell animation? That's a piece of the process animators used to make cartoons. For every second of cartoon goodness on Saturday morning, they had to paint the characters in progressively different poses at least fifteen times. For really good animation, like Disney movies, there would be 24 cells of animation drawn and painted. For TV animation, there would be something like 14 to 18 cells.

The cells are sheets of clear celluloid. The animation team would paint an image on each one. They would then put the cell on a pre-painted background and shoot it on one frame of film. They would then take that off the background and put the next frame on and repeat the whole process. It took thousands of drawings to create a half hour episode of the Smurfs or the Carebears (the classics). This process has been superseded by computer animation processes. There is no need for cell animation. But that does not mean the cells of past cartoons are gone for good.

The reams and reams of cells were thrown out or left to rot in warehouses. They are now bought by weird guys who want to remember their childhood. They want a piece of their childhood. I know of one animation collector who amasses all the cells from the X-Men cartoon from the 90s. He can look at a cell and tell you what episode it was drawn for. I guess it pays to be a savant if you want to collect obscure elements of antiquated animation methodology.

For the most part, because there were so many cells created, they don't have a huge monetary value. You want some Bugs Bunny cells? That will cost you. If you are in the market for Strawberry Shortcake animation, you might not break the bank. They are berry affordable.

The other piece of information you will need is, who is Godzooki. When I was a Saturday morning cartoon devotee, in the 70s, there was a Godzilla cartoon show. Godzilla was a good guy, saving the world from giant monsters. But you can't just have a giant monster to sell sugar cereal, you need a funny sidekick. Godzooki was born. He was a diminutive relative to Godzilla who was silly and always underfoot. Oh, that Godzooki. He even made it into the theme song. He was legit. I thought he was great, though if he is recalled, it is with derision. He is the Scrappy Doo of the Kaiju world.

And I have several cell animations of him. The cells show a great deal of work. They were never meant to be loved for themselves. They were always part of a whole, of a cartoon. But this is how you can get close to the shows you love. You can own the smallest of parts.

I have a small collection. I have some Ewoks cells and a Charlie Brown cell that was part of a Chex cereal commercial. They are fun. They are a reminder that entertainment takes many steps and many hands.

But I think I am being a bad collector. I read that I am not storing them correctly. They are made from celluloid. They can deteriorate. They will start to break down and a strong vinegar odor will come from your disposable art piece. There is a name for this, it is called Vinegar Syndrome. It is deadly to the cell. But I'm not concerned. My cells are smelling fine, for now.

But that's the thing with disposable art. Do we want these to last forever? Is art meant to be eternal? Is the art that brings nostalgia even worth preserving for the greater world? Or do we all know that soon we too will turn brown and blurry and smell of vinegar? Will all the memories of our childhood ooze into simpler parts? And who will sing the praises of Godzooki then?

Update: *The collection has grown somewhat since I last wrote about it. This time, I picked up preliminary drawings that were used before the cells were drawn on and then painted. I have production drawings from the animated video Hulk vs Thor and I have a few drawings for the Snorks. These were rip-offs of the smurfs. They are Smurfs, but they are under water. When I bought the Snorks art, the woman at the That's Entertainment said, "Thank goodness you are buying this. It saves me from buying it myself."*

Twenty Five: Unplayed Video Games

My son and I were in a large Antique shop where he found a bin of old video games. He had to look at them, they were video games after all. They were older XBox and Playstation Games. We don't have the latest systems, but the previous versions. However, the ones he was focusing on were older than that.

Eventually, he found two Rainbow Six games from the earliest XBox model that he wanted. They were three bucks a piece and he looked at me. Can I get them for him?

"Okay, I can get them for you," I said, "but you can't play them."

My son gave me the look of disappointment only 13 years can give their doddering parents. "No. You can only play this on a first generations XBox or one of the new XBoxes which they say can read all the old models."

"And we have neither of those, right?" I asked. I really know nothing about video games. Despite my hope of being a cool parent, I am just about useless.

"But we will have the new system one of these days, when it is not so hard to get. But I should get them now anyway."

And that's how we now have in our collection of video games, two new obsolete games that we cannot use. It is the art of the things that do not work the way they were supposed to. One of them has the manual for the game. I guess that's something.

There has been a big swing for older video game systems. People are in love with their Atari 2600s and their first generation NES.

Some of the games are quite expensive. Now the part that gets me is that you can get the games graded and they will be encapsulated in plastic. You can't get it out without great effort. So here we go, paying great money for a game that you do not plan to play. It is a totem. It is a symbol. You don't have to learn when to jump or who to shoot in this game. The only way to win is to have the money to own it. It is conceptual art.

That's not what we have here with my son. We have a game he will play, or hopes he will play. Plans to crack open like a pesky nutshell. Then the fun will start.

We have unplayed games at home. Everyone does. These are the games he was excited for, but after playing them for a while, discovers that they are just not fun. Eventually, they will be sold or traded, but now they are the unused reminders of non-preferred entertainment.

My son is not sure if he will ever play them. "I hope to. But it's three dollars. It's kind of not a bad bet." Oh no. I sure don't want my son talking about bets and gambles, let alone really laying down a two dollar bet on the ponies somewhere down the line.

But the comparison is apt. The unplayable games are just like getting a bet on the Mega Millions. You don't really think you will win, but you are paying for the joy of imagining how great it would be to win that much money. In the same way, these Rainbow Six games are laying a three dollar bet on future excitement. It might not be an exciting game, but the anticipation is worth the money. The dream is always worth putting the bet down.

On our shelf are not two more obsolete games, but two more pieces of joy and anticipation. Every shelf should be stocked with such things. We should be filled with dreams of what can be. It is Schroedinger's First Player Shooter. Spin that on a console, why don't you?

Update: *We now have a system that will play those old games. I asked my son if he has played them. "Not yet."*

Twenty Six: Ugly Ties

For several hours on Sunday, I wear the ugliest ties I can find. I walk down Millbury street on Sunday afternoons, heading to the poetry reading I run at Nick's with the most heinous examples of ties. They are wide. They are made from petroleum. They are louder than a car horn. I strut down the street with pride. The peacock walking the walk.

The amazing thing is that I get compliments. People tell me they love my ties. They are happy to see such a blast of unpleasant art. One nice fellow told me that my "tie game is always on point." This was never my intention, but I thank them sincerely all the same.

When I run my poetry reading, I always wear a tie. I want to hearken back to the old ways of dress. Also, I have a lot of ugly ass ties and I figured I should use them. The poetry reading seemed like the easiest victim for my sartorial crimes.

Here is the thing, some guys are hard to give presents to. The old stand by is the tie. I am not sure why. I have been in education for almost my entire adult life and the parents of my students, if they felt the need to gift me anything, gave me ties. I have a lot of pro-education ties.

I have ties from my son. The first birthday gift he picked out and bought by himself for me. He was so proud. He wanted to make sure I was wearing it. Even now, when I put it on for the poetry reading, I always make sure he sees I am sporting it. He nods his approval.

Then there was the year I sold insurance at a place downtown. They insisted that all male employees wear ties. Sure. Okay. They said ties, they never said pleasant looking ties. When I got the job, I went on a quest in all the discount stores for the ugliest ties in existence. I think I met the objective.

So now I have thirty or so ties of questionable taste. Some seem to be created by designers who have never understood color. They are garish. They are childish. They rest around my neck with relaxed aplomb.

Now, even back when I wore these beauts during my Insurance selling days, people would give me compliments about them and I would wonder what was wrong with them? Or what was wrong with me for not understand the inherent beauty of the clashing tie design? Am I the one with no taste?

I don't do anything to spruce up the tie. I don't put it on a nice, dry cleaned shirt. I wear sneakers and jeans. I am that pretentious middle aged guy who thinks that a tie with blue jeans means I am hip. The younger folk can relate to me.

And what are these ties? We have a tie showing crayons. There is a child's drawing of ice skating. The one with the hundreds of polar bears. They might be polar bears. They could be mutant lemurs. We also sport geometric shapes and colors. Baby, we got colors. I have one tie that clashes with itself.

The question we must ask, when did anyone think these ties looked good? Did they gaze upon this polyester abomination and say, "Yeah boy, that is one snazzy beast."

Was there a time when we blessed the loud and ridiculous? Did we believe the adage that the wider and uglier the tie, the better the man? Is that the equation we have?

It's sad to see my poetry reading ending for a variety reasons. One is that I will miss the reading. The other is that I will not have any good excuse to wear this menagerie of neckwear. I will have to start another art event, just so that I have a reason to look ridiculous.

With the second to last poetry reading today, I put on a new-old tie I picked up for two bucks at a thrift shop. We think it might show pine cones, but are not sure. I put it on and placed a hat on my head. I asked my son, "Is this good? Does this work?"

My son looked at it with a critical eye. "Yeah. It works. Everything works with an ugly tie."

Twenty Seven: Second Hand Bed Sheets

Here at the Library of Disposable Art, we celebrate the things in our lives that we keep that no one else sees as valuable or worth holding on to. That's all well and good. But what of the items that no one would ever perceive of keeping.

There are some things we cannot conceive of preserving. Once we are done with it, we throw it away. There. It is gone. But hold on, buckaroo. Everything gets resold. Even used bed sheets. Yes. Bedsheets. The things you sleep in. Those things. Maybe they shouldn't be resold. But they are. And people are making decent money out of it.

We know of a local reseller who is now cornering the market in this type of product. There are a lot of types of items that people pick up cheap at thrift stores and garage sales and then resell on Facebook Marketplace or Instagram or EBay. There is also WhatsApp and Mercari and Etsy. People sell because people want to buy.

And they want to buy bedsheets?

Yes! They want to buy bedsheets.

Our Thrifty Contact was being a little vague on some of the details. She didn't want to tell me where the honey holes are for finding bedding. There are certain thrift shops where the good designer sheets lie in wait.

Our Thrifty Contact worked on clothes, getting them beautiful again. Getting them salable again. Nothing looks good bunched up on a rack in a GoodWill. But you can fix it and make it lovely once more. That is what she loves doing.

But the truth is, she ain't the only game in town. Other thrifters are out there fighting over the good shoes and the designer jackets. There is some fierce competition on these things.

Not so much the bedsheets.

Some people are not interested in dealing with material with such a dirty past.

But our Thrifty Contact has no fear. She saw quality. She though she could sell it.

She learned out to take the yellow from pillow cases (Hydrogen peroxide in a spray bottle. Hit the pillow case and then let it dry in the sun. Repeat until pretty once more.) She patches things up. She cleans them and irons them. No dirt. No wrinkles. Ready to sell.

She did admit that as soon as she went into the World of Bedsheet Retail (TradeMark Pending) she bought a black light.

Why? Why would you need a black light on second hand bedsheets? I have really no clue.

Our Thrifty Contact would not answer my question. She only shook her head and added, "There was one set of sheets that didn't pass the black light test. That got thrown out. And you are welcome world."

She has put out very nice sheets and made a good profit.

That does not answer the question of who would want to spend decent prices for used bed sheets.

There is an intimacy to the sheets you wrap yourself in during your most vulnerable moment of the day, when you are asleep. These sheets are our protectors, the warmth of mothers.

Do we want someone else's sheets? Would they be as pretty and welcoming as a brand new set?

When we are asleep, and filled with dreams, as long as they are clean and pretty and comforting, we will always give ourselves over to the good grace of the bed sheets.

Update: *My friend who supplied me with the information on this one and she felt I got it pretty much right. I could not ask for a better endorsement.*

Twenty Eight: Etch-A-Sketch

1- No one ever bought an etch-a-sketch for themselves. This was not one you ran to the toy store for. This was not on your want list. No. The Etch-a-Sketch was always an unasked for gift. This was something an aunt would give for a birthday or it was the back-up Christmas present. Santa himself liked it well enough, but even he would not give it pride of place under the tree.

2- The line you see when you move the etch-a-sketch is not what you think it is. It is not something added to the screen. It is about removal.. The line you see is an absence.

3- The screen of the etch-a-sketch is coated with powdered aluminum. You control a stylus that scrapes off the aluminum powder. You are not seeing a line being made. You are seeing the trail of aluminum being pulled away. The art we create is a negation.

4- This was a big toy when I was a kid. It was big in size (to my tiny hands) and it seemed that every kid had one. That might have to do with all those aunts out there desperate to give a present. Though not as popular as it was in the 70s, the etch-a sketch is mostly seen as miniature. You can get it for a couple bucks. It fits in your palm. It is attached to a key chain. It makes very tiny masterpieces.

5- The etch-a-sketch was originally called the Magic Screen. It was invented by a French engineer named Andre Cassagnet. I mention this because it is important to remember that the toys we played with were created by someone. Someone had to develop it. Someone had to go out and sell it. Someone had to believe in it enough that they wanted it to be ignored in every playroom in the world.

6- The thing about the etch-a-sketch is that you cannot stop your drawing. It needs to be one continuous line. There is no break to a drawing. So you would draw a house where the doors are connected to the windows. The car had wheels attached and let's not even think about the passenger side door. But that's okay. None of this stays. Everything in the gallery of etch-a-sketch is temporary.

7- If the drawing you created is awful, you simply take the whole etch-a-sketch, (which is the drawing and the canvas) and shake that sucker for all it's worth. Shake. Shake hard. This is not a simple swipe for erasure. You have to put a little aerobic force in this act of disappearance.

8. Nothing lasts in a etch-a-sketch. It is made to be shaken to memory. Good thing. Who can make anything worth remembering with this damned thing anyway?

9. You can watch a video online of Princess Etch. She is a professional etch-a-sketch artist. She makes intricate renderings of many things: from Sailor Moon to the Taj Mahal. She charges anywhere from a few hundred to a few thousand dollars for the etch-a-sketch. She makes the image permanent by removing the aluminum powder from its shell. But that seems against the point of etch-a-sketch images. The money and permanence. That is not what we love about an etch-a-sketch. We like to shake it.

10. Isn't that what we want over all? To shake things hard and then they are gone? To have all our little mistakes covered over by a shower of powdered aluminum? Had a fight with your partner? Shake that moment like a etch-a-sketch. Told off your boss? Shake that like a etch-a-sketch. You get lost walking over to your friend's going away party? Shake that whole day. Make it start again, where you are sure you have now mastered the knobs and gears.

11. The impermanence is not a design flaw. It's why we keep on coming back to make the next messy, continuous, object of brilliance.

Twenty Nine: The Gentle Art of Crushing a Beer Can On Your Head

In the 1979 movie, Animal House, John Belushi crushed a can of beer on his forehead. The can collapsed into a condensed ring of aluminum. The scene showed a drunk, slightly bored, Belushi bring an empty up to the center of his forehead and apply force. It folded into itself.

Is this where it all began? Was this the scene of drunken fraternity ennui where the fad of crushing the beer can began. Is this the Ur moment of beer can crushing? Or was this always something that people did?

Is this a type of physical punctuation? If the drinking of the beer is the sentence, then what you do with the empty can is the punctuation. If you put it in the trash, then that is the period. If you hold up the empty for a friend to see hoping they will give you another beer, then that is the question mark. Crushing the beer on your forehead is the exclamation point. It is the full throated statement of being.

Maybe the crushed beer can is part of a lost ritual. Not that lost, because cans have only been around since 1935 and there is no way anyone would want to crush those four ounce steel models. This is an act created by the change of material. No one would want to crush a beer can if it wasn't made of aluminum. We will only want the illusion of strength. Not the real thing with all that collateral pain included.

Which just brings us back to the question. Why does anyone think that crushing a beer can on your head is a cool thing? Are you trying to be John Belushi? Do you want to emulate a comic actor who died at the age of thirty three of substance abuse?

There are numerous articles and youtube tutorials on how to crush a beer can on your head. Of course there is.

The first one I viewed is the one I will describe. I saw one. Do I really need to see more? The video featured a young man in a Chicago

Blackhawks jersey. He wore a mohawk and explained that the other beer can crushing tutorials are wrong. They advocate using your fingers to put dents in the middle of the can. Don't do that. That's not what the purists do. "Everybody shows you how to cheat, nobody shows you how to do it properly."

Will there be a regulatory board that will approve the beer crushing action? Will they look at some beer crushing events and label them heretical?

The mohawked Virgil took us on this three minute tour of his can crushing inferno, with the statement, "The trick to this is really simple, like basic physics." Like basic physics. That means that beer can crushing is "physics adjacent."

"You have to hit it hard enough where the can takes the impact." This makes no sense. But we are talking about crushing a beer on your forehead. This is not about sense. This is top down, 150 mph, screaming into the wind. This ain't no disco.

He pointed out the places on the head that are the hardest. Ram the beer can there. Use a flat palm. Use force. You will not feel a thing. Like basic physics. Basic physics makes your head numb.

His first attempt was only a half crush. He explained that his finger got in the way. He did it again to show that even experts can make mistakes. It was more crushed. It was not as flat as the film record of John Belushi, but how can you even attempt to replicate greatness?

The video was instructive and let me know how to do something I will never do. Like reading a 1930s Popular Mechanics on how to make my own television. I am not going to do it. And I don't want to. And I'm okay with that. The world is strewn with half finished homemade televisions and beer cans ceremoniously crushed flat.

It is our job to navigate around all the detritus.

Update: *I wrote this for another project. There is a series of books about mundane things called Object Lessons. A few years back I decided to write one of these 25 thousand word books and try to sell it to that* series. Beer cans were my subject. I wrote a good amount of it before my interest petered to zero. I forgot about this abandoned project but one day went through it and found this essay there. It was easy to excise it from the manuscript. I am happy there is something from that project that was able to be published.

Thirty: Cake Breaker

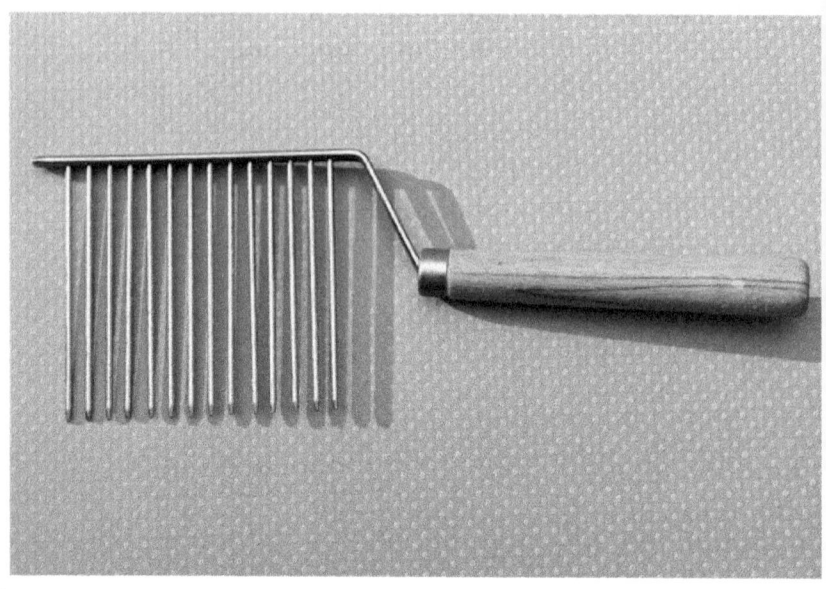

Before we go into why people collect certain things, let's figure what the hell we are looking at. This picture can be unsettling to contemplate. What the hell is that? Is this for dog grooming? Is it for people grooming? Is grooming involved in this in any way?

This item has a decorative handle. The handles can be different. What is always the same are the 13 to 18 closely spaced cylindrical tines. That's what makes this thing what it is.

Okay, what the hell is it, then? Well, if you read the title of this column, you will know that this bad boy is a cake breaker.

That is one of the coolest names for a utensil ever. You don't get words of destruction in most of your utilitarian kitchen objects.

I can almost imagine that a cake breaker would be a large wooden mallet that was wielded by a crazed food critic. The mallet would be slammed on the offending cake and frosting and filling would splatter on all available walls. It would be the sweetest crime scene. You can see it on the latest episode of CSI-Patisserie.

Unfortunately, that is not the case.

A cake breaker is a device made to cut delicate cakes. All of the sources I looked at only give angel food cake as the one example of a delicate cake. I am sure there are other delicate cakes feeling slighted right now.

I am sure anyone attempting to cut a piece of angel food cake would like this kind of device. It was created to not smoosh the cake down. It creates a decent slice. And to some people, getting a decently presented slice is tantamount to godliness.

Personally, I just rip-off a chunk of cake with my hands. I think that is the best way to deal with such deserts. I don't need the proper cutting device. And I don't need to wash the knife or breaker later. See, I'm always thinking. Being a neanderthal has its advantages.

We actually know the history of this device. It was patented in 1932 by Cale Schneider of Ohio. What necessitated him to climb to the pinnacle of utensil greatness? Was he at a luncheon with the wife and watched the disaster of cutting up a delicate cake and realized that something must be done and he was the man to do it. .

Now that you know what it is for, look at the picture again. Doesn't it make sense? Isn't it an elegant solution to a real (though minor) problem? Someone used science to come up with a better cutting device.

The amazing thing about it is that it adheres to Louis Sullivan's axiom, "Form follows function." To know it's purpose, it makes sense. But if I didn't tell you what it's function was, you would have to say that this was an instrument of destruction. You might say that it was used on naughty children who always forgot to brush their hair. "Your hair is a tangled mess, now I will teach you a lesson by brushing your hair with the cake breaker."

Just so you know, we are not recommending you use a cake breaker to comb anyone's hair, even if they were naughty. Silly rabbit, cake breakers are for cakes.

Thirty One: Text Pages in Old Comic Books

I was listening, last week, to the most unheralded form of fiction, the text pages in old comic books. Let me explain a wee bit.

Back in the forties and fifties, comic books had several pages of text stories in them. This is not because they wanted to class up the joint with prose, no. They were forced to by the Man. The government demanded it.

In order to keep the very important and very cheap postal rates that magazines got, they had to have a certain amount of text only pages. The government would not give mailing discounts to picture books. You had to have words.

So, if you ever get to look in old comic books from that bygone era, you will find that everyone has prose stories. What were the stories like? Who knows.

No one read them. They bought comics to look at funny pictures, not to read stories. Reading stories was a school activity. But the stories were there, because they had to be.

Most of the stories were written quickly. They were not good and they didn't have to be. Because no one was reading them, there was very little need for quality.

Struggling writers sent their oft rejected stories to the comics text pages. They paid poorly and you didn't get a writer's credit.

Nothing says disposable art more than the least cared about part of a larger piece of disposable art. The unwanted section of a comic book. It is the greatest hiding place in all of literature.

The other day, I downloaded a collection of Space Patrol stories by Otto Binder. These stories were first published as the required text pieces in Captain Marvel Adventures in the late 40s. These stories, following one intrepid Space Patrol member, were published for years.

And now I was reading them. I was breaking the oath and reading comic book text pages.

Actually, I had my Alexa read it to me while I drove to work. I had a fake voice read me unwanted stories. Perfection.

The stories are basic science fiction drivel. The hero does heroic things. The aliens are either evil or misunderstood. Sometimes they were both.

My son was in the car and he asked me about these stories. "Are they supposed to be this bad?" I first took offense. They are not bad. They are cheesy fun.

But instead of getting defensive about my reading choices, I said, "They aren't bad. They aren't good either. They were made just to be there. To fill up space. And for that, they are terrific." My son shrugged and decided that I was an idiot.

Update: *For most of the time I wrote this column, I was not involved with the publication of them. I would write them on a shared file and my editor would pick the one they wanted to run that month. They never told me when they were to be published. I wouldn't pick up the Worcester Magazine every week. Sometimes I would see my work in there, sometimes I had no clue. So I don't have any clue which pieces were published or not. I guess I could go through the archives online and check, but that seems like so much ego. The one column I was sure was not published in the magazine was this one. I wrote it and put it in a file that was closed. I wanted to write it, but I didn't know if it was going to do well in publication. This one was written just for this book. I am sure we are all so proud.*

Thirty Two: Bookmarks

The bookmarks hang around the house, mocking me.

Yeah, bookmarks are mean.

They are not just the rigid piece of rectangular paper that let's you know how much more you need to read before the end of the chapter.

No. They are the Greek Chorus of Literary Derision. They are laughing at your ass.

While putting books away on overstuffed shelves, I invariably come across some book that has a bookmark in it. It's a reminder that here is another book I have not finished.

The book mark is that silent nudge that pantomimes laughter at my inability to finish a damned book anymore.

What with streaming old TV-Shows, to watching YouTube videos on how to make money from dryer lint, to my editor's important instagram posts, who has time for reading anything more than a menu on the DoorDash app?

But the bookmarks look on and smirk their papery smirks. And it makes me blame myself. Why didn't I finish that book?

Was I distracted? Was the book over my head? Was it too simple? Did it have too many words? Was I so taken with the beauty of that last read paragraph, there was no way for me to ever continue to the next page?

I might want to start up the book, but it might have been months since I read it, and I have no idea what is going on and so I have to start from the beginning.

And there is the presence of the bookmark. You can almost hear it say, "It looks like you won't need me here. I guess I'll have to go back to Chapter One. Oh well."

Sometimes the bookmarks are really sneaky. They are showing in a place of the book I haven't gotten to. Many times, a good bookstore will put their own branded bookmark in a book. I will discover it and realize that I have not read to this part, I haven't even started.

Do books feel better with bookmarks placed deep into the volume? Are they hoping the other books will think of them as ones of those "Being Read" books? As opposed to the books that just gather unopened dust.

Bookmarks are mostly pieces of advertising. They have the logo of independent bookstores. If you have enough books, you will be greeted with the sensation of seeing the bookmark for a shop that went out of business. You hold that piece of paper like it was a fading echo.

Or they will have a quote from a kinda famous writer about the joys of reading. You will have Einstein's opinion on reading, as if some of that genius will rub off. Or if not him, a picture of Hermoine Granger reading. "Books are Magic!"

Of the kiddie bookmarks with the yarn tassel on top. They show Snoopy or Heathcliff. Some bookmarks have punny jokes on them. Like the kids want to use bookmarks with Dad Jokes written on them?

There are shmancy bookmarks. They can be 3D or be a signed limited edition bookmark from a favorite writer or artists. Bookmarks can be high art. It's profound and it helps me not lose my place.

I will often use whatever paper I have around. Magazine subscription cards have been used as bookmarks in this house. And receipts. I am repurposing those insane pharmacy receipts. I'm upcycling.

Not so long ago, I was going through a book and found a receipt from Tower Records, from around 1998. And if I read anything in that book, I have no memory of it.

I do like bookmarks from bookstores. It is a journal of where I went for my books. The places that gave the secret password. There are books here. There are stories to take home with you. Don't worry about not finishing the story this evening. You can mark your place. You can put a flag down as if to say, "I was here."

Thirty Three: Stickers and Where to Put Them!

At first, there was the door to a high school locker. A long metal expanse that was virgin and unspoiled. The inside of the locker door was a private surface that you gazed at several times a day. Such a dull drab thing to stare upon and contemplate all the vagaries of a high school existence.

You might as well decorate it. Pretty that dull ass door up!

You could cut out pictures from Sports Illustrated or Tiger Beat Star and look upon all the craven idols, like Joe Montana or Scott Baio (oh so dreamy.) But that takes work finding the picture, cutting out the image and then taping it down. It's exhausting.

That's where stickers come to rescue.

Now you can put all of your anarchy on the metal canvas with aplomb. You can put some Wacky Pack stickers, or the ubiquitous Garbage Pail Kids. You are showing that you are gross and you also thumb your nose at mass commercialization.

What if you don't want to go to the corner store and pick up a pack of Topps stickers? You can get a sticker of a band logo. Anthrax. Megadeth, Air Supply. All of those crazed bands your parents and teachers despise.

You don't have to like the bands, or even have heard of them, but putting them on the locker door shows you have some adhesive cred.

"Why do I have a Masters of Puppets sticker in my locker. Well you know me, I love puppets. Kookla Fran and Ollie and all the Muppets."

The art for the sticker is not yours, but the placement on the locker makes you the artist none-the-less. You are conductor. And everyone is happy. Except for the Janitor at the end of the year who had to scrape all of this discarded art away. Damn kids with their need for personalization.

Now you are an adult, or pretending to be adult-esque. Do you have any surfaces that need the sticker treatment? What parts of your world are filled with void? And emptiness that needs filling?

I am not the one to know. I never use stickers. I put a Garbage Pail Kid sticker on a notebook I was writing a novel in, and then thought better of it. Did I really want my writing to be defined by the shambling image of "Dead Ted?" So I don't know why adults buy stickers.

So, I asked online and got the obvious answer I was unaware of. They are used to adorn water bottles and laptops. People like to sticker up the things that are lugged with them wherever they go.

Now, I am sure most of you will hear that it is water bottles and laptops and wonder why I didn't know that. WHat's wrong with Dave that he writes about crap he has no clue about. Of course, if you have read even a tiny bit of my writing, you will know that I never know what the hell I am talking about. IT's kind of my thing.

People want to make these things their own., So they buy stickers and place them in funny locations on the bottle. Or they will get that sticker from that nice Nordic Death Metal band (such nice boys) and display on the laptop for all to see. This is not a safe sticker and you are not a safe person, and it is important for everyone to know it.

The stickers decorate our drab parts, but they also give us a chance to define ourselves the images we pick.

She has kitten stickers on her bottle. He has lots of Marvel Superheroes on his laptop. We are the mass produced images we chose.

The stickers are a pain to take off. You can scrape them but there are traces remaining. It's best to just throw out the bottle and the laptop and get new ones. New canvases for what you want to be seen as.

Thirty Four: Dirt (But Spooky Dirt)

There was a magazine (if I have to explain what those are, we are all doomed.) called "Famous Monsters of Filmland." The magazine featured stories about those well known monsters and ghoulies in film(land).

But let's not worry about that now.

Let's trouble ourselves with the ads in that memorable magazine. To be more precise, let's look at one ad from 1979.

This was an ad for jewelry. Don't run away, we know that the boys who read these magazines are not cool with jewelry (or bathing) but sometimes there is the coolest of pendants on offer.

Like this one. This was a pendant in the shape of a coffin. It was see thru, so you can see what is inside. And you will see a gram of the purest dirt.

Not just any dirt. It is dirt from Dracula's Castle. That's right. This ain't dirt for no mud pie. This dirt got itself some pedigree.

This is real. The ad says its really from the castle of the one and only bloodsucking, peasant impaling Dracula himself. Accept no alternatives.

This dirt is pure evil. I am sure the writers of the ad would be happy to do a Pepsi Challenge that this dirt is good shit.

For 9.95, plus shipping, you get the coffin shaped pendant, you get the dirt, you get the band. You get the whole evil glory of the vampire. Ten bucks in 1979 was no joke. This had to be the real thing, because they wouldn't charge that much if it was fake. You see. I'm using logic here.

This pendant is the ultimate conversation starter. Without something as universal as a pendant filled with dirt, our boys will never talk to girls.

Some people actually responded to the ad's posting online and reported that there actually was dirt. Where does that dirt come from, who can say? It could be from Transylvania, or the Universal backlot or maybe from your backyard. It's a big yard and I bet you have enough dirt back there to fill a thousand pendants.

Other people who sent for this collector's item stated that it was cheap and bargain basement as hell. The pendant was plastic and pretty flimsy. If you were not careful, the thing would break and you would have to vacuum up all that precious vampire soil.

But there is something endearingly charming about a boondoggle that doesn't hide the fact that it is so damned fake. You have to love the obvious liar.

One person who commented about this ad said they have the pendant hanging on the rearview mirror of his car, like he is warding off creatures of the night or people with better judgment.

The ad says it comes with a certificate of authentication. And no one can make up a fake certificate, no sir. The copy states, "Not a gag, not a spoof, not a gimmick, not a put-on."

But what if what we want is a gag, a spoof, a put-on? What if we want to believe in the spooky dirt. That the pendant is not plastic. That the dirt is more than common dirt. That the world is stranger and more fashionable than we could possibly believe.

We find the talisman that works for us. It might say we are a disciple of the dark lord, or or it just might state that we love chintzy silly things. We celebrate the macabre and the uselessly ironic.

You have to admire the maker of this geegaw. He showed amazing supernatural powers. He took a gram of ordinary dirt and made it important. Valuable. Worthy to hold on to.

Thirty Five: Do Not DIsturb Signs

At the Nova Park Hotel in Switzerland, the Do Not Disturb Sign, shows a hippie girl, amidst the swell of some foreign flora, with her finger to her lips and she is saying, "Psss't." At the top of the card, where the doorknob goes, it says of the hotel, "where people get together." Okay. Now we know what they are not wanting to be disturbed from.

One of those places.

One of the great things about staying in a hotel room is the ability to control your privacy. You have the opportunity, nay, the right, to put the little doorknob hanger out and let people know that you are busy. You are making out with a friend. You are finally finishing the chapter in the book you are writing, you want to eat that oversized piece of tiramisu by yourself. Whatever the reason, you can tell the employees of the hotel to "bug off."

Many of them give you the opportunity to turn the sign over and let them know that you have deigned to accept them into your abode. They may now give you clean towels. Aren't you just swell?

Who invented this amazing piece of pop art? Who came up with the sign on the door knob that let the world know that you busy being busy? Or that you are wishing you were busy being busy and this is just a ruse. You are misusing the power of the do not disturb sign. Sometimes you just have the word type. Or you might have a picture of someone sleeping in. They always look more at peace than you do.

One sign has a singular sheep staring at you. The type reads, "Counting." That maybe is a little too outre. You don't want conceptual art on your do not disturb sign. This is a utilitarian piece of art. It has a purpose, and you really shouldn't obscure it with conceptual art concepts.

There is something naughty about collecting the "do not disturb" signs. You are taking it from the next customer. You are robbing the next room guest the ability to be left alone. You are the person stopping an extra hour of sleep. You are evil. Quite evil.

How is it done? Do people collect all the do not disturb signs from their stays at hotels? Or do they go out of there way for rare do not disturb signs. Do they go for that 1974 Hilton Tokyo sign that all the collectors are fighting over.

Are there such things as rare and collectible do not disturb signs?

Let's stop and praise the collectors of single pieces of paper. It has got to be one of the smartest things to collect. You can put them in boxes or binders and they are easy to store. Collecting strangely shaped items, like beer bottles or shampoos from around the world, you are going to have to figure out the space issues, because that will happen quite fast. Having pieces of paper is the best kind of collection, even if you are not so excited about the subject matter, you got to love the fact that it is easy to store.

So maybe these collectors of paper will cast a large net for their desired items. This leaves us with more questions than answers. Why do collectors want something so utilitarian? How do you become a collector of do not disturb signs? And is there any cure (for this collection as well as the summer time blues)?

But there is no way to find the answers. The solution is to ask a collector of these paper reminders, but we can't. The door for the collector has a sign on the doorknob that says, "Sleeping, come back later, will you?" And who are we to deny the power of the sign? Okay. We'll come back later. We're good like that.

Update: *This was the start of the end. I was running out of ideas. I was having such a hard time coming up with things. I came up with this one by searching online for "weird collections." This one worked for me. But it also told me that this column was not going to last forever.*

Thirty Six: The Map of Disposable Art

This is where we go local.

This is where we celebrate the places around us where we can find odd and wonderful things. Where is tomorrow's disposable art hiding out?

In the nearly three years of writing this column, I have been fighting the good fight in discovering and writing about a variety of items I have found. In the beginning, it was easy to do. I had a wealth of things to write about. In other words, I have a lot of crap.

But now we are around thirty installments of this silly thing and coming up with topics is not as easy as you would think. We are surrounded by disposable art, but realizing it sometimes is a challenge. These little knick knacks, these curios are so ubiquitous that singling them out for discussion is a hard task.

When stuck, I might put into the internet machine, "weird things people collect" and then I am off to the races. That is how I discovered that people collect Do Not Disturb signs.

That is not the ideal way to discover these things. Not just to write about, but to collect and enjoy. I am not only a chronicler of disposable art, I am an addict. (Don't worry, I can stop anytime I want.)

So we get to the big question for the day, where do we find these delightful, useless things?

For me, one of the great emporiums of cultural detritus is That's Entertainment on Park Avenue. Let me tell you something, you don't have to like comics and Magic the Gathering cards to have a good time.

It's a large sprawling warehouse of pop nonsense. You have comics and cards, sure. But you also have wrestling magazines, LPs, Garbage Pail Kids stickers, Japanese snacks, posters and the occasional head scratcher. I remember stumbling across old menus for a cruise ship there. I didn't get it, but I am just happy that such ephemera is around and able to take home with someone who understands how cool it all is.

Like all the best treasure sites, the more you dig, the more wonders you uncover.

Crompton Collective is a great place to find a gift for someone. They have some booths still selling antiques and curios and you can find an occasional glass doorknob or a 100 year old sled. It takes a little searching, digging, but things can be found.

In the same building is the crazed Stem to Seed. You can get flower arrangements. You can get taxidermy. You can get polished rocks. That's a place to linger in and let your eyes focus on the well curated madness.

For me, my favorite place to recharge my disposable art batteries is south of town in Uxbridge. It's kind of a sclep to get to, but the Bernat Mills antique mall is a place I always find something odd and inspiring. We have gone from old video games to ugly ties. The place offers such a variety and there is a lot of it.

But these are just the places I go to. There are sprawling flea markets in Grafton and Hubbardston that always produce stuff you ain't never seen before. "What the hell is this thing, anyway?"

I am sure you can tell me of your favorite junk stores and thrift shops. What places work for you? Where you find things you never knew you needed?

Or you can eschew the trip to shops and just dive into your attic. What things have you kept? What photo albums and boxes of trinkets are still waiting for you to bring to light. Blow the dust off and soak in the joys of keeping things that mean the world to you. They are only valuable because you make them valuable.

Or maybe you will find these priceless artifacts on the side of the road. Dumped out of a window. Or waiting for the garbage man or the ersatz dumpster diver to come across it and declare it worth keeping.

Treasure is everywhere. Close your price guide apps and open your eyes.

Update: *I enjoyed writing this one immensely. I loved writing about the local. I wanted everyone to discover the weird shit you can find in Central Massachusetts. What a joy to find such useless treasure. All of the locations I mentioned are still in business, which iis a wonderful detail to admit.*

Thirty Eight: Gin and Tonic as Seen as Disposable Art

Eight years ago, I created a blog project where I attempted to go to every bar in Worcester and then write about it.

The idea was to understand why people go to certain bars and avoid others. What makes a bar yours? Also, I wanted an excuse to go out and get a cocktail. (like you really need an excuse)

But it wasn't just your shot and a beer. No. I had rules of engagement. I was to always pay in cash. I would never ask for top shelf ingredients. I always asked for the bottles in the bar well. I would have one drink and leave. And that drink? A gin and tonic (which would have been obvious if you read the title to this column)

Why did I pick a gin and tonic? Because it is simple. Four ingredients and that's all: gin, tonic, lime slice and ice. But these simple ingredients made a world of difference depending on where you got it.

Some of the gin and tonics were good. Some were awful and sickly. One place was a giant glass of ice. One pull at the straw and you finished the drink. There was one restaurant (not around anymore) where the drink tasted of ashes. I couldn't figure out how that happened. It was a mystery with every sip.

One bartender didn't know how to make one and after some discussion she gave me a drink. It was gin and coca-cola. And part of my rule to this project was to drink everything I was given. So I did. What I do for my eager readers.

I had a gin and tonic made for me by a one-armed bartender. He had to open a new bottle of tonic for my drink. It took some time for him to finish making it, but I never had a drink that was made with so much deliberation and care. Perhaps it was not the best cocktail, but it was an honor to drink it all the same.

And there were some superior gin and tonics that took my breath away. How did they take these same ingredients and make something superior to all the other joints? Two of my favorites are still around and I will be happy to mention them: The Fix on Grove Street and Basil n Spice on Shrewsbury. I don't know what made them so damned good, but I was in awe.

The cocktail can be considered the greatest of disposable art. You put disparate liquids into a glass and bade someone to drink it. You can admire the taste, the aroma, the way it looks in the glass. And then you make it go away. Skol.

You can have complicated cocktails with obscure elements. You can whip up egg whites and include them in the melange. You layer the liquors to give it a striped image. You can light the cocktail afire.

But the real talent is doing none of that. The real talent is taking simple elements and making it taste perfect.

How can gin and tonic in one person's hands be a disaster and another, a thing of beauty, a joy for all time?

The care. The knowledge. The type of glass used. There are so many factors to a creation of art instead of doggerel in a glass.

You got the drink. Does work for your needs and your wallet. To it please the eye. Does the bar itself please the eye. Is the stool comfortable? Does it work for your belief in the world? Is the music good? Does the place smell of desperation and cheap beer or does it have the odor of autumn leaves and kindness? And who are you having this humble drink? Is it for business or do what to be here? Do you have faith in the surroundings that made this drink for you?

That's the key there, friend? The amazing thing about a good cocktail is that everything other than the drink matters almost as much. You don't get more ephemeral or more disposable a piece of art than a well made gin and tonic.

Once, an older bartender gave me my drink and contemplated it, as all good bartenders do. "A gin and tonic," he intoned. "I like a gin and tonic. In the summer. Gin and tonics are summer drinks. Perfect for the sunny afternoon. That's when I like it." He stopped and craned his neck to see the slushy roads and the snow drifts outside the bar's window.

He looked at my off season drink and smiled down at me. He forgave all philistines such as myself. We would never understand beauty if we keep gulping down art in the wrong season. In the wrong cup.

Let's face it, friends, all bartenders are artists. They make wonders with flair, and sometimes with a garnish.

Update: *The book is available for sale online, Gin and Tonics Across Worcester.*

Thirty Nine: Drift Glass Memory

On a shelf of an old bookcase, in a Vermont junk store, I saw four old Milk Of Magnesia bottles and thought of my grandmother.

They were large, all displaying the striking blue that was part of its image. The blue bottle. Do people even use it anymore? It was for upset stomach and constipation. Don't we use other things for that? Are we not impressed with a cool looking bottle anymore?

Looking at them, I was gifted a memory of my Granny. She spent her last thirty years in Ocean Gove, New Jersey. It was a shore town with one of those boardwalks that Bruce Springsteen crooned about.

We would visit her every month. Her house smelled of age and salt water. On Autumn days, when the crowds thinned, she would take us to the beach where we made sand castles and she looked for beach glass. That is what she called it. But I guess the standard term is drift glass.

She found some white pieces and a couple pink ones. She displayed them on her hand and explained how it became smooth and opaque from years and years being hit by the salty waves.

The salt and the water were the sculptors of such beautiful creations. They took the shards and made them lovely to look at and to hold in your hand. There is a gorgeous tactility to drift glass.

She explained that this was made from litter. People throw there bottles into the ocean and eventually they broke into shards. Only when they were in shards did they have the chance to be such lovely things.

I recall Granny being excited once because she saw a flash of blue on the tide line and ordered my sister and I to investigate. She wanted to know if it was blue sea glass.

We came back to report that it was just a candy bar wrapper. Granny was disappointed. "The blue one is dear. You hardly ever find the blue glass. That's because there aren't a lot of bottles that are blue. Milk of Magnesia. That's it. And you hold on to that. That keeps in the medicine cabinet for years and years. And then it goes in the bin and not into the waves. To find a piece of blue glass is lucky day. Things go right when you find one of those. Oh, aye. They are the prettiest things to find in the sand."

I never thought of the scarcity of subtle glass pieces. I wondered how to get more blue drift glass. I came up with a plan. Collect all the blue bottles I can. I would have to get hundreds of them. Then, when I had enough, I would break them into pieces and dump them a few hundred feet from the shore in Ocean Grove.

I couldn't put sharp pieces that hadn't been blunted by the waves right there on the shore. I couldn't have people walk the shore line and come out with shredded feet. No. I was being kind in my big picture plan.

In a year or two, the blue glass would be drift glass and my grandmother would be able to find it on her walks.

I never did the plan. Of course not. I never shared the idea with anyone, because even as a kid, I was aware of how dumb an idea it was.

But today, landlocked in Vermont, I spied the four Milk of Magnesia bottles and was giddy with the notion that I should buy them, break them up and plant them into the churn of salty water.

And just like forty years before, I denied the urge. It was just another bad idea.

The bookcase these bottles reside on used to hold novels because there is still a sign on the top of it that reads, "Fiction." In some ways, with the memory of these bottles, it is still selling fiction. Or at least, daydreams.

Forty: Glass Eyes

I blame the bar Vincent's for this foray into disposable art. Yeah. Blame an excellent bar. Don't blame the writer. You see, I was trying to come up with a topic for this month's column and I thought of all the amazing, and odd, taxidermy specimens at Vincent's.

Hey, I thought, I could write about taxidermy. But then, I started an online search and found an image of a hundred year old ad where a company sold taxidermy and glass eyes. Now, glass eyes are important for taxidermy, but it seemed they also were selling glass eyes for humans.

And like that, I asked the question that most are too squeamish to ask, "Are there people who collect glass eyes?"

And the answer is.

Yes.

Were you expecting any other response?

Of course there are people who collect glass eyes.

Someone is selling a 1900 circa glass eye collection for over three grand,. That doesn't mean someone will buy the collection at that price, but hey, now we're haggling.

Glass eyes were difficult to get in Europe after World War One. There was not enough raw materials to make the very precise eyes, and there was also a great need for them, what with all the veterans who last their eyes and their innocence in those foxholes. You have a classic limited supply with a big demand kind of situation. Someone with a lot of glass eyes were sitting on a gold mine.

Luckily, the raw materials were available from America to make the glass eyes needed. More than enough, because more wars wer coming.

There is still a great need for artificial eyes, but they are not made like these artisanal items. These were hand made by young women (with small hands) and each were individually designed. Nothing was off the rack at the Nordstrom's Medical Supply Store. Glass eyes are not "ready to wear."

But I can make glass eye jokes all day, but that does not answer the question, who wants to have a glass eye collection?

Is this a morbid thing? Is this what the grown up goths collect when they are done with their Tickle Me Ed Gorey dolls? Is this just to be a kind of Wednesday Addams wannabe?

Or do the collectors find something important in their display of glass eyes. Because you have to remember, these were not made for display. These were made for a socket. Someone had your collectible in their head.

There is a heaping spoonful of humanity here. This was very intimate. They say eyes are the windows of the soul. What vista does a glass eye open up to? Does having this collection of castoff facsimile organs offer a sense of the profound. Can you be closer to one's own mortality by gazing into these unseeing eyes?

Years ago, I had eye surgery. I had my cornea replaced. It was great to have happened, but it also creeped me out. This cornea I got was not made in a lab or blown in a kiln. No. This came from someone. Someone who had aspirations and dreams. And now a part of them was deposited into me. I still think of this unknown hitchhiker. The houseguest that doesn't leave. I am grateful. I am also weirded out.

The glass eye collections that I saw online also have that aura of being extremely personal. There is history in these. There is heartache and pain in every glass eye. And you have to gently dust them every few weeks so they can continue to shine.

Forty One: Gum Gardens

On the questions-and-answers website, Quora, someone asked a question that no one has bothered to ask, "Why do people like to stick gum under desks?"

There were a good deal of answers to this query. Most of them said that the people were apes, or lazy jackasses or awful people who ruin everything for everyone.

I am sorry, but I was unaware that the idea of gum under the desk was so triggering for a large amount of people (of course this is a self-selecting group of folk who actually respond to Quora questions, so they might all be a tad high strung.)

Is laziness a factor? Maybe. I was a lazy gum chewer who could not bother disposing of gum the proper was, which was to put the used wad in a wrapper and fold it securely only then may you throw it in a trash receptacle. Oh boy. Too much.

But I wouldn't put it under the desk. No. That's crazy. I did it the right way, I swallowed it.

Does that mean I have a large deposit of flavorless gum in my stomach, taking up real estate? Despite the word on the street (or the school hallway) that is not true. According to the Mayo Institute, the gum is not digested, but it leaves the stomach and heads to other places.

Part of the problem with the gum gardens on the bottom side of desks should not be completely laid on the lap of the kid.

Some of this falls on the teacher. The rules were never clear. Some teachers said you could have gum but "do not chew like a cow." Or that you may never have gum in school and Juicy Fruit is the forbidden fruit from the Tree of Knowledge of Good and Evil.

So no gum? Got it. Have to do it on the sly.

But then there were some studies that proved gum chewing helped kids focus on lessons and tests. So you can chew kids, but only if it is academically warranted.

And I have heard teachers dispute this and say that gum in order to do well on the MCAS exam is just so much hokum. They don't care if they are told to do it, they are not letting these mouth breathers anywhere near chewing gum.

Yeah, Kids don't know if they are chewing the things that will make them a better student or just so much contraband. It's best to hide the evidence no matter what. And so they put it on the back of desks.

And what happens is a collection of gum shapes that harden with time. Can the gum on the bottom of desks be considered art? Absolutely.

You might say that there was no plan or intention to create something that is art, but the doesn't stop it from being interesting to look at. Some might say that gum gardens are disgusting, but that is a sterling recommendation for it being considered art. It evokes an emotion out of you.

You might say, "It's not art if my kid can do it," and that is apt because it was probably your kid that did it. I saw him with that pack of Wrigley's. He is the culprit, and the artiste.

Look, we now can see graffiti spray painted on walls and call it street art. Why can't we look at gum gardens and call it, School Detention Art? Why must we deny the beauty just because the Man is against it?

I am sure there was a kid who looked at all the gum he left under his desk and thought, "This is too monochromatic and does not really pop," and so they decide to chew another color of gum just for the aesthetics. Secret, hidden art is still art, my bucko

I would love to see the Worcester Art Museum do a show of Gum Gardens. They could hang the desks from the ceiling and we can walk under them and admire the art of accidental creation with a craned neck.

Of course there are a lot of art critics and school custodians who don't see this as a good thing. The best way to remove the art, I mean gum wads, is to hold ice on it until it hardens and one can break it off easily. And another artwork is gone to the ages.

The custodians and the gum chewing artists have something in common.

Both call the other Philistines.

They are both right.

Forty Two: Joke Shops

I met a man who spoke highly of being a kid in Worcester in the 60s. Downtown was a good place to hang out and be a kid. He told me about the candy stores and the other shops, but his favorite was the joke shop.

"That's the place you went to get the can that had fake snakes jump out." He told me this as if to make sure that there were such places as joke shops in the world.

The name of the joke shop is incorrect. It is a prank shop. In this world, there is an ocean separating jokes and pranks. Though there comes moments when I am not sure the difference.

You need plastic poop. This is the place to go. You want a candy box that is really a mousetrap. Well, step right up kid, don't be shy. It's all flim-flam. It's all just stuff and nonsense. Kayfabe for the rubes.

The man I was speaking went on, "I would be given a little bit of money to get something after school. I guess I could have gone to the candy store, but I always went to the joke shop. I would get the garlic chewing gum.

"It was garlic because it was supposed to taste awful. You were not supposed to like garlic. And it really was garlicy. I kind of liked it. If there were still joke shops, I would get a couple packs of garlic gum."

That's the secret of any kind of success. That something was meant as a joke, but instead you turned out to like it a lot.

I kind of like to think of that young kid from the 60s going to Elm Park to play, with a mouth reeking of garlic.

I have to wonder what was the purpose of the joke shop?

To be goofy of course.

But there was something more to it than goofy, there was an edge of anger in the products. From the sharp taste of garlic to the severe vibration of a joy buzzer that makes you think you are being electrically shocked. These are not innocent japes. There is a sense of malice. Of transgression.

The joke shop was a place to thumb your nose at the Man. And of course, you can buy a fake thumb at the shop. I mean, do you even have to ask.

For me, I remember ordering a few of these from the back of a comic book. They always disappointed when they arrived. They were never as good as I imagined them to be. Of course, at a joke shop, you would see that the items were lame, and you would still buy them.

I don't know if the plastic poop or the joy buzzer will make a comeback, but I have high hopes for the resurgence of the garlic gum. It can't just be one kid. There has to be thousands of people who want that earthy, pungent taste as they try and fail to blow the biggest bubble in the world.

I don't know how, but let's make it a thing. Bring back the Garlic Flavored Gum. Free it from the ghetto of the joke shop and get it in the regular, respectable convenience stores. Only the best late night shops stock Garlic Gum. Try it. You might not like it. But you might.

Forty Three: The Word Faith

I was talking to Ken today. He manages the pop culture emporium, That's Entertainment and he always has time to give a kind word to customers and writers of odd magazine columns.. He was telling me of one of the new trends for comic book collectors. The high end comics have gotten so expensive, collectors can't afford a complete copy of many desired comics, such as the first appearance of Thor in Journey into Mystery #83 from 1962. Not without getting a second mortgage on the kids (I mean house.)

There is a new thing you can do. You can buy just one page of the comic. If the comic was ruined over the years and is incomplete, then people can break the book. They separate individual pages of the comic and get them authenticated and encapsulated in hard plastic. He told me they had a partial copy of the first appearance of The Joker (Batman #1 from 1940) and one of those pages went for a lot of money.

People can't afford the whole comic, but they can get one page. Ken is excited about this new market in comics. He has incomplete comics he couldn't sell, but now that he divided them into pages, they can make some money and give collectors a chance to possess them. . I have a problem with this. I don't like the idea of breaking a book down into parts, even if the condition is pretty rotten.

He told me about another example that he came across. On an auction site, Ken saw someone selling a word written in Abraham Lincoln's hand. Someone took a large piece of writing by Abrham Lincoln and cut it down to single words.

What is that word? They were selling the word, "Faith."

Ken thinks that it was probably a dull letter he wrote in his capacity as a lawyer. Maybe he was looking for payment and wrote something like, "We are looking for good faith payment." That is something a lawyer might write.

And now, for sale, online was that one word. Out of context. We don't know what kind of faith he was talking about. It can be any leap of faith. As long as it was written down for all to see.

This fascinated me. People want a little bit of the figures they admire. Lincoln is one of those guys we all want something of. You can't afford a war era letter by him? Get the word "faith." Believe in the word "faith" that it actually was written by him.

Provenance has always been a major issue. Looking at a random word, you have provenance issues all the way up to the Penthouse. But faith is not just the word on the auction block, it is the way we need to proceed in buying it. Faith that the word "faith" is Lincoln's. That the hand we believe in formed these letters. It is less artifact and more totem.

Ken told me that he didn't bid on it, but now has regretted it. He saw the Lincoln movie and suddenly had the urge to own a word written by the man. He told me that if he did buy it, he would have it in a large two foot by two foot frame and there would be a matte with only that word showing in the middle of all that blank space.

Can you imagine leaning into the framed word and reading "faith." Someone would have to tell you who wrote that word. Someone would have to tell you what it all means.

Forty Four: Birthday Corsages

I was visiting my mother in New York, and she told me of another disposable type of art. Birthday corsages. This was big when she was in school in the 1950s.

The idea was that for your birthday, your friends would give you a corsage that you wore for the day. The more corsages you had, the more popular you were.

This bothered me. "What would happen if no one gave you a corsage. You might not want to go back to school again."

My mother waved that off. "Oh, you always made sure your best friends gave you the right kind of corsages for your year. You planned it an you would get three or four and any more would be a bonus. The really popular girls would have seven or eight of them. They would be covered in birthday corsages."

She told me that for every year, there was a different kind of corsage. Most of them were made from candy. For your tenth birthday, you wold have lollipop corsages. Gumdrops for your eleventh. Bubblegum shows up for thirteen year old. Sugar cubes for sweet 18. Lemon Drops for the Sour 17. (What the hell is Sour 17? Is that a thing?)

And for the 14th birthday, the girls received a corsage made of dog biscuits. That was to symbolize puppy love. I think the makers of this tradition missed the basic concept for puppy love.

This was a good part of the business plan for local New York florists. They didn't just make wedding bouquets and flower arrangements. They made sugar cube and dog biscuit masterpieces. There was no mail order lollipop corsages. These girls kept their kitsch local.

My mother did not mention the 18th birthday corsage to me, but research showed that it was made of beer bottle caps to show that this girl is legal to drink. There is so much disposable art weirdness wrapped up in this one. Did the girls drink the beers ahead of time to collect or did the florists keep a healthy supply of Blatz beer caps on hand to please their customers?

This was a thing of the past. No one does it anymore. It certainly is not a popularity contest, which is a good thing. There are people on the internet who want this to come back and be a thing once more. I am sure some of those proponents are owners of flower shops.

My mother was rosy with nostalgia as told me of these mementos. Of course, she didn't have them anymore.

"I loved the ones I got for my 14th year, the dog biscuit year. I wrapped them all carefully and put them in a box and placed it on a shelf in my closet. A few months later, when I was feeling blue, I decided to look at them. I opened up the box and all of these bugs came out. There were bugs everywhere. Not a lot left of the corsages. I screamed and ran from the room. I didn't really like the tradition much after that."

Forty Five: Air Sick Bags (Halloween Edition)

In my quest to find interesting disposable art, I came across the odd vein of collecting that is airsick bags. They do go by another more alliterative name, which I will only use once. Barf bags. Okay, I cleared that out of my system and I will happily call them air sick bags.

So yeah. There are a good deal of collectors for air sick bags. Some of them can go for a good deal of money. Of course they are pricey, because all the ones collected have never been used. I worry about the collector who has "used" examples in their collection. (To my dear editor, I don't know why the last few columns I have written are all kind of gross. I guess that's where we are in the survey of disposable art. We have gone through the fun ones and now we are left with the more unsavory examples. Oh well.)

The collectors of such ephemera have a lot to work with. Air Sick Bags were made in over 200 countries for hundreds off airlines. They all had their own designs on this piece of airplane equipment. Some of them are quite good looking. Some are fanciful. They were ubiquitous.

It makes one wonder how awful air travel was in the first half of the 20th century that it was required for everyone to have a bag with them in case they are sick. That's a hell of a lot of turbulence for an entire industry to create a bag that is used for one thing and one thing only. This is not a bag you see lying around and think, "I need to put my lunch in a bag, ah, here's one. And look, the sandwich fits perfectly in my air sick bag." Words that were never written before this moment.

With all the problems with air flight, it is probably easy to say that most air sick bags were never used. They just sat there in their place in the pouch in front of the passenger and wondered what the purpose for their existence could possibly be? They are there just in case the improbably would occur. Like the guards in front of Buckingham

Palace, they stand there silent and straight just in case a terrible event might happen though it never does.

Now marketers knew a good thing when they saw it, in the form of a bag.

There is a long history of horror movies giving out air sick bags to audience members before they went in. There are a bunch of movies that did this including such classics as Blood Feast, Cannibal Ferox and the Beyond. Now, it is just a rumor but I have heard they also gave out the bags before people entered the most recent Indiana Jones movie, but I have not been able to confirm it.

The one that got me was a Halloween one. This was made by a Southern Church. It has the image of a jack o'lantern witch hybrid flying on a broom with the words saying "Halloween is Sickening to God." I think this was meant to be handed out to trick or treating children instead of candy.

Okay.

Let me just say that there are times when I don't understand people.

This, of course, is a terrible idea. Why would you do such things to kids? It is a terrible idea and I hope that it was never done. I hope the only one that exists is in the Barf Bag Museum and that no kid had to be assaulted for having fun on October 31st.

It's stuff like this that makes me sick to my stomach. Maybe I do have a use for the bag after all.

Forty Six: The Letterlock Paper Football

What is the most common use of origami in America? I have an opinion that is probably wrong, but I am going to run with it and this is my column and I can be a dumbass if I want.

Origami is just the art of folding paper, changing it to three dimensions. With that definition, I think the biggest form of origami in America is the paper triangle football that we played with during school lunch.

Do you remember these?

You would fold a piece of paper into a slightly robust triangle and fold it in a way that it didn't have any paper dangling and then you can...Play Ball!

If you don't recall, you played with another kid on the other side of the table. You had to flick the paper ball to the other side of the table. If you got it hanging over the edge within three flicks, you won the touchdown. If it didn't make it to the edge or it toppled over, you did not win the drive. Then you would kick a field goal by flicking it again through the fingers of your opponent.

I don't know how I would have gotten through all those endless cafeteria gulag sessions without playing this game. You don't have to like sports to be playing paper football.

The history of this underground American pastime is that it began in Madison, Wisconsin in the early 1970s.

I am sure there are leagues and many, many rules variations. I am shocked that there isn't a show on late night ESPN2 for this. Hell, this is as exciting to watch as cornhole, so let's make this happen!

The folded paper triangle is a great ball, but it also was a way for soldiers to say, "I am alive. I am okay."

I know, that was a big swerve in the narrative, but stick with me

I was talking to someone who's mother came from Moscow. She told of these folded paper triangles. They were letters sent from Russian soldiers during World War 2 back home.

They would write on one side of the paper and then carefully fold it into this triangle. The paper became the outside envelope. This was a method of folding a letter into its own receptacle called letterlocking. This was saved on paper.

The soldiers did not have to pay to send a letterlocked triangle. It was sent to the address free of charge.

Sometimes there was very small tight words telling a long story, Other times, there was just a simple signature. It didn't matter what was written when one of these came home, because all of them were saying the same thing, "Don't worry, I am still alive. For now." The paper triangle was the Sign of Life.

It should also be said that letterlocked pages were easy for government censors to check to see what was written. The censors didn't have to rip open any envelopes. Anything to make the lives of censors easier.

For us, we might see something from our youth. A fun game to play in the cafeteria. For older people coming from Russia, they would see something else. Something that says and means more than any touchdown run can ever be.

Forty Seven: The Kiddie Picture Dilemma

A crayon drawing of a cow that actually looks like a broken end table. A finger painting miasma that apparently is a portrait of mommy and daddy. Cotton balls glued to a blue piece of construction paper with the idea that what we have is a lovely afternoon sky.

These are just some of the art projects that your children bring home from school or day care. They show you with beaming smile and runny nose. They are so proud. And so are you.

You hold it in your arms to admire it. You put it on the fridge with magnets. You frame them. You tape them up in the hallway like they are the Van Gogh on loan from the Louvre.

One of the great things about having kids, the art they make and want to share.

But there is a problem.

It doesn't stop.

The art comes.

Almost every day, more art comes home.

What to do? You will drown in all that construction paper and biodegradable paint.

It is a slowly rising flood of pre-school art.

This ain't stopping until they discover dating or video games.

Sure you love your kids works or art, but dammit, there is a metric ton of this stuff.

When I worked in a pre-school, I once got a desperate note from a parent begging us to not send the daily artwork home with the child

There is only so much space on the fridge. There are only so many walls to cover with the drawings and the paintings and the collage and the (what the hell is that, don't ask out loud, just smile and say you love it).

But this is a real issue. What do you do with all that creativity that your child has presented to you?

For us, wwe have a large box in the attic over teaming with art projects. We never look at the box, but that thing ain't going anywhere. It will last longer than the sun. We also have a few favorite pieces up on the wall. I am looking at a clay bas relief our son made at Worcester Art Museum. It is proudly in the dining room.

But is t his how everyone does this? Does every family have an attic full of coloring book pages?

So I asked my friends this question. For the long haul, what do you do with all that art? Al l that art center beauty?

Many of my friends used the term recycle the art. That is a kind euphemism for tossing it in the bin. Many recycle it. A few scan them and have them on a flash drive.

Others pick their favorites to frame. If something comes home that is amazing, they replace the old framed work with the new one. They are looking for examples that really show the child's progress or personality.

One of my favorite responses was by the wonderful Worcester poet, Eve Rifkah when she wrote, "I saved a few special things and tossed the rest. Though in the tossing, it was nice to sit a moment and recall that time in my son's life. Too much becomes a burden."

Our children are butterflies. They are not the reason for us to be hoarders.

As far as I know, we kept everything that came back from school. There will come a time when a culling will be in order. Something to lighten that burden. It will not be easy, but we cannot be weighed down with all that paper and promise.

Of course one of my friends had a different experience with the whole issue. She wrote of her three children's art, "Burned when the house burned down."

Forty Eight: Used Wedding Rings - Cut in Half

This column has become a series about things. Item. Stuff. The things you keep with you. The things you don't want to get rid of. This is a series of the hangerson. We revel in the detritus.

But today is about a thing that I do not carry about me, but is still necessary to me. It is about my wedding ring. A ring I do not wear anymore.

I am still married. But I do not have the ring. My finger is bare.

My wedding ring was a used band from the 1950s. We bought it from an antiques jewelry dealer I used to work for when I was a kid.

I am a writer of forgotten things, of disposable art. Would you expect me to buy a brand new ring? The engagement ring I gave my wife and our two bands all came from the same dealer. They were all sturdy and beautiful. They were also affordable, but that is beside the point.

I wore that ring without fail for 16 years. And now it has been nearly two years that I haven't.

The ring is not missing. I know where it is. As I write this in my dining room, I can see it. It is in a doctor's specimen cup.

I am sure you are thinking, "Oh boy. I suppose there is a story about this."

And you would be correct. There is a story.

I used to drink. Whisky mostly. There was a time I drank a lot of Gin and Tonics, but that's not the story we have here.

I was a weekend drinker. And I had a hard time stopping at one or two.. One drink meant the day was gone

I knew this was not what I needed. I tried to stop and was successful for a spell. Then the lockdown happened and I was back and worse than ever.

Finally, I created a dumb compromise. I wouldn't drink unless I was away. I was to be a vacation only drunk. I did say it was dumb right?

I would go every few months to Brattleboro, Vermont to write and to drink. I wrote a good deal on those weekends. I drank more.

So it came in January. I was up there and I drank a lot and I did not black out, but my memories of what occurred that weekend are ephemeral at best, like watching an intricate dance through a shower curtain.

I was back at work on Monday and my hands were bothering me. They were itchy and really uncomfortable. I was scratching at them and that made them swell up. Or they were always going to swell up and the scratching just made it worse. I don't know what I did that weekend that caused the hands to swell like that. I was close to freaking out.

By Tuesday, my hands were so swollen I realized I could not get my wedding ring off. I went to urgent care. They asked me what I had done to get my fingers so swollen. I said I could not recall.

They told me that if I wanted to keep the finger, they were going to cut my wedding ring off. They said that jewelers could mend the ring, but for the meantime, the ring had to be cut off.

I cried watching them slowly (damned slowly) cut through the ring. After a half hour, my finger was released. They put the ring in a container they had about, a specimen cup. They reminded me that the ring is not ruined. It could be fixed.

But I haven't gotten it fixed. Almost two years, it sits in the specimen cup. Because in that time, I have not drunk at all. If I am tempted, I will look at my bare ring finger.. Or if I am quite challenged, I will go over to the specimen cup and shake it and hear the ring rattle like the bones of a forgotten friend. Everyone's sobriety is individualized and kind of kooky,

This column has become a series about things. Item. Stuff. The things you keep with you. The things you don't want to get rid of. But other times it is about the things we chose to not have with us. What does the absence say about us? How can the things that are missing still make us whole?

Wedding rings are the symbol of love fealty. But they are not forever for we are not forever. All rings are used rings. All rings are cut in half if you look at it from the a clear angle

When I got home the day from urgent care, I showed my wife the specimen cup and teariily apologized to my wife. She smiled and told me, "The ring isn't the marriage. IT isn't what makes us love one another. The ring is just a ring."

Forty Nine: The Unwanted Posters

About 20 years ago, I was at a fundraising auction to raise money for a poetry event and I won a vintage 1950s movie poster. It was for the movie "The Pusher/" Guess what he was pushing?

It had a great silhouette of the trancoated drug pusher and some over the top ad copy about the horrendous world you can see in this movie.

Man. I loved that poster. I got it framed and it was one of the first things I hung in my condominium. It stayed with me for years.

I loved this thing. I never saw the movie, because it was hard to find, but if I could get it, I would watch it. It was based on an Ed McBain and I found a copy and have read it. Well. Most of it. I get the idea. Drugs are bad.

There is something weird about being a completist like this. Just because I have the poster to a movie doesn't mean I have to be an expert on it. I just have the poster on my wall, not because I want to give you a lecture on the publication and film history of "The Pusher" but that it looks neat and I am the kind of guy that demands neat stuff on the wall.

It was up on the wall when I met and married my wife. It was on the wall when we brought our son home from the hospital.

When we moved out of Worcester to a nearby town, the poster made it too and was on the wall. For years.

Then our son got old enough to read and didn't like it. It bothered him. And then we were having play dates for him and we realized that the movie poster for Pusher might give a wrong impression. Yes. Wrong impression.

So it went up the attic to a corner with other pieces of art and framed posters that no longer meet the standard of display.

There are a few more pieces that might be considered "Risque," There are now a lot of framed prints of fairy tales images that were hanging in our son's room. They were too childish. They were not cool.

So we have an Elephant's Graveyard of Unwanted posters. They were great when I was not married and wanted to show my ironic nature. Now there are about a couple dozen forgotten pieces of wall capable art that are stacked like so much cordwood.

And now we go through it again with my son's room. It still has prints of lions we got for him at Start on the Street when he was little. There are a bunch of cute pieces of art.

But he is now a teenager and he does not want cute. He wants posters of Pink Floyd and Black Sabbath. He wants posters of fighter jets.

And we begin the processes of changing it from a room that was decorated for a child to one that is designed by an older individual. Ah well.

All of those pieces of art will now make it up to the attic and the Elephant's Graveyard of once cool images.

Perhaps we should release them into the wild. Let them be free. Or, donate them to Savers. But we just can't seem to let them go. The art is something that might come around again. Maybe there will be a time when my son won't be embarrassed by my "The Pusher" poster.

Paul's Second Letter to the Corinthians says there is a time to give up childish things. But I have to ask. Why? Why must we give up childish things? They are nice to look at. They fill up the wall. There is age inappropriate joy hidden in all of them.

Fifty: Cardboard Wallet

In sixth grade, our class was given one of those forms where we can order books and magazines, all to make us book hoarders and possible readers. The book company gave us an incentive for everyone who ordered more than three dollars, a wallet. I don't know why, but the kids in the class were excited about getting the wallet. Actually, this was going to be my first wallet and I was kind of psyched. What a wallet had to do with purchasing kid's books is beside the point. It was a free wallet! (with purchase)

It was a long month before the books came back from the company. The teacher reluctantly gave out our free wallets. He did it, but it was in the most half-hearted of gift giving. The wallet was a piece of cardboard that came with directions so that we could fold it into the shape of a wallet.

Most of the kids were pissed. They felt ripped off. They wanted a real wallet, the kind made from the skin of a cow for our three dollars of books, not a lousy piece of cardboard. The teacher sagely suggested that we write our displeasure to the company. He suggested we can work on our letter writing skills.

One kid said, "This is my letter of complaint," and he ripped up the wallet into little pieces. He then took a large envelope on the teacher's desk and put the pieces into it.

This was followed by other kids ripping up their wallets and tossing the fragments into the manilla envelope. It became a thing. Everyone ripped up their envelopes into itty bitty pieces. It was a moment of twelve year old rebellion. It was out middle school streaming of the Bastille.

And then everyone had destroyed their cardboard wallets. Except for me and one other girl. She said she wanted to keep the wallet and received a chorus of pre-adolescent jeers. I was not brave enough and I ripped it up and tossed the remains in the envelope. I was not happy with myself. I wanted the wallet, even if it was lame. It was mine and I knew I should have kept it unmolested. It was a piece of crap, but it was my piece of crap.

The funny thing is that now people who lean toward the green are trying to make cardboard wallets a thing. It is animal safe and surprisingly durable. There are scores of videos on how to make this DIY life hack. You don't have to pay money for a wallet when all you need is cardboard and some origami skills. Some videos state that theirs were designed by paper artists and you will create a work of art as well.

But to me, the great piece of art would have been not following the crowd. Not bowing to the pressure of the group. I probably would have hated my cardboard wallet, but if I did rip it up, I wish it was my idea. My choice to do so.

I wonder what the teacher did with the envelope filled with the detritus of ripped up customer premiums. Did he keep it with him in his desk until his retirement? Did the next teacher find t he envelope in the desk and wonder what the hell this is? Why did anyone keep a manila envelope stuffed with ripped up cardboard? What is the purpose of keeping such unexplained destruction?

Fifty One: View Master

1- The View Master is a stereo viewing device that came out in the 1930s and was very popular for years. You put your eyes up against two viewers (one per eye) and see a stereo-sort-of-3d image.

2. You would get the View Master, but you would also need to purchase individual the reels for them. You might get a reel package of the Grand Canyon or Snoopy and the Red Baron. The choices were endless. Well. Not endless. There were a lot of them.

3. For the first few decades of its existence, it was not a toy. This was a piece of film viewing equipment, me bucko. This was a way to see wonderful vistas and breathtaking sites in kinda 3D.

4. The reels were serious shots of landmarks and famous places. View Master reels were sold not in toy stores but in the gift shops of famous places. You go to the Lincoln Memorial gift shop, you can get a View Master reel instead of a postcard. Postcards don't have dimensional qualities. Of course you can't just slap a stamp on a View Master reel and send it to your Aunt with a comment of "Wish you were here."

5. It was only in the fifties that the focus expanded to the kiddie market. You had a Charlie Brown, Jack and the Beanstalk, the Flintstones, among many others. But these were not just pictures from the cartoons. No. No. No. That is not sophisticated enough for the erudite View Master Audience. They replaced the drawings with dioramas of the characters.

6. Yes. The dreaded diorama. The bane of my 4th grade existence. The little sets and the characters that are then presented in class for a grade. In this case, they were photographed for the View Master reels. Why would they do that? Why would they make the Flintstones live more in the uncanny valley then they already do?

7. They made these simple drawings into weird dioramas to show off the 3D effects of the View Master even more. But to me, it always

creeped me out to see the little clay Charlie Brown try to kick his plasticine football.

8. Did every kid in my neighborhood have a View Master? Possibly. But did we ever use them more than once or twice? Not a chance.

9. Already, the need for this type of technology was fading. It went from a personal way to look at sighte and places and then became a toy for kids and then turned into the gift your distant cousin would give to you.

19. A few weeks ago, I sent a friend a picture of a View Master viewer I saw in an antique mall and he texted back that it was ancient VR.

11. Which is ironic, because about a decade ago, the owners of the View Master product tried to go into VR technology. Yeah. That was just a Hail Mary pass for technological relevance.

12. As a kid, I pined for the Star Trek reels. I knew that if I was ever to find them in Toys R Us, and then convince my mother to get it for me, my life would be complete.

13. I am still waiting for the sense of personal completion. I wonder what that diorama would look like.

Fifty Two: Old Irons

People collect flat irons. Of course they do. Why would we expect anything different? People collect old shopping lists, why wouldn't they collect old irons.

Irons have been around for nearly a century. Any foundry in any small town would make them up. The first kind was the flat iron or sad iron. Sad iron? Is there a prescription they can take so they aren't sad anymore? I would much prefer a medically induced peppy iron, thank you very much.

Actually, sad was an old English word for the concept of heavy. That makes sense that sad is heavy. When I am sad, I feel the weight of the world on me. When a friend tells you the sad story of woe they are going through, you would say, "Man, that's heavy." Just think of how more interesting the movie Back to the Future would be if Marty McFly used the correct old English in the scene when he said, "Doc, are you telling me that my mother has the hots for me? Whoah, that's sad."

Anyway, let's move on, because we have a few more irons in the fire.

The idea of the iron was that it was a heavy and solid piece of iron that, when heated in a hearth, would keep the heat and work for some time. The French had the idea of a hollow iron, thinking that it would heat up faster, but the problem was it was too light and light irons don't retain the heat. Silly French!

It was only until 1880 that the first electric iron showed up. The steam iron was invented in the 1920s.

This is where the collecting of irons gets complicated. There is a difference between antique and vintage irons. Antique irons were made when it was just a piece of iron. The ones before 1880 are antique irons. The electric and the steam irons that are old are vintage. Confused? Well iron out the folds of your brain and let's move on.

When I was a kid, my mother taught me to iron. It was necessary. I really sucked at it. I would create more wrinkles when I was done then were there in the first place. I never taught my son how to iron, because people are now living in wrinkle free clothing.

So what do we do with the antique iron now? It can be a doorstop or a paper weight. You can straighten out your frizzy hair. You can throw it full force at an acquaintance wondering why you own so many useless things.

I think the issue I have with collecting irons is not the iron itself. It is our hatred of wrinkled clothes. Why do we discriminate against wrinkles, be it on linen, cotton cloth or on aging faces?

Why are we so keen to get rid of wrinkles? To place a white hot piece of iron on it, eradicating the innocent wrinkle that was just there minding its own business.

Shouldn't we consider the wrinkled shirt a real piece of disposable art. Look at the way the wrinkles create vistas and valleys. Why should we get rid of them. Shouldn't we celebrate the simple American wrinkled dress shirt? Throw away your sad irons and wear the shirt the way that the cloth wanted it to be. The cloth wants the wrinkles. The cloth makes the wrinkles. Don't disparage the cloth, baby. Let your wrinkled flag fly.

Fifty Three: Jelly Cabinet

You can find a jelly cabinet in Crate and Barrel. Or if the annual trip the IKEA. You will be able to find that two door storage cabinet that your dining room is missing. People will want to eat in the dining room if you had a jelly cabinet.

But what is a jelly cabinet?

Why are we burdened with generic furniture that has such precise names?

It is a midwestern piece of furniture that showed up in the 1830s. It was a way to hold on to your jams. There was a lot of fruit and you needed to preserve it, so you made jams and preserves. You would have the cabinet lined with blueberry jam or raspberry compote. (I don't know what a compote is, but I have seen it mentioned a lot on the Great British Bake Off)

The shelves were designed to just hold jars.

It could also hold pickling jars. So if you also had too many tomatoes that season, you could pickle them and keep them in the jelly cabinet. Did the pickled cucumbers get annoyed that they were in a Jelly Jar? They were proud vegetables, wouldn't they want to have a Pickle Shelf? Is that too much to ask?

I have a question about the fact that the jelly jar was in the dining room and not the kitchen. Was this something cool to have while eating? A cabinet filled with jelly? Would you stop in mid meal to sample the jams? The more jelly jars you have, the more wealthy and important you are in the community?

It is hard for me to see jelly and jams as something to display in the dining room. It is something you buy and use half of. I have so many unfinished jars of preserves in the fridge. We buy one, thinking that we will use it every day and then get tired of it in under a week. Was the traditional jelly cabinet also a hangout for unwanted preserves? Did they look on hopefully every time the cabinet was opened? Maybe this is the day they will remember that Strawberry Jam is great on toast! Please!

Now it is a utilitarian piece of furniture with just a funky name. It was used for jelly jars until that faded from fashion. Then it was used to hold CD music collections. The shelves were perfect for that. When that left fashion, the shelves were converted to hold DVDs and BluRays. When streaming showed up, we got rid of the discs and now that cupboard is once more bare.

It is still a nice piece of furniture. You can store all the different kinds of coffee you are into. You can make a craft cabinet for the kids. It can hold china and all that good crystal you got at your wedding and have never used once.

There are a lot of uses no matter what you call it.

But every now and then, when you use it, you are haunted with the feeling that the shelves are slightly sticky. Put your sticky finger to your lips and you get the afterimage of something sweet. Something that was meant to be there.

Fifty Four: A Tub Full of Baskets

Who doesn't love a woven basket? They are the perfect thing for a table. Woven Willow Baskets. Woven Hyacinth Baskets. Baskets Made of Seagrass. Rattan Baskets. There are so many beautiful things that make these baskets.

And what do we do with these baskets? We put rocks in them. Or artificial fruit. Or seagrass. Or real fruit. Or potpourri. Or towels. Or soap. Or towels and soap together in a great team-up situation. Or hard candy. Or pine cones. Or bottle caps. Or matchbox cars. Or whatever grouping of things you want to hold in one place and maybe think you should display because it looks kind of cool.

We are the prisoners of the design magazines. They tell us how to make a room pop. They inform us what simple things we need to make our rooms feel whole. To make ourselves feel whole. You need a splash of color. You need to counteract the negative space. You need more negative space. (And just so you know, I am not a hundred percent sure what they mean when they say negative space.).

And that's where the basket comes in. You can put something in that basket and fill up all the space and loneliness you and the room are feeling. You will be more accepted by your family if your room has some simple accents that emanate pumpkin spice. Bring on the basket. It can be a thing of beauty in itself, but you really need it filled with interest and intrigue. Whatever did the Michaels put in their basket? I am not sure what they did, but it held the room together.

And the basket has a handle which makes moving it about the room or the entire house even better. If there was not already such a thing as a basket, then the home decorators of the world would have had to create it.

Even though Pier One Imports has gone into the color coordinated model kitchen in the sky, there are still places that push for interior design. There are many interesting things that they encourage you to use to spruce up your house, but no one is going to get rid of t he decorative basket. It was born to hold your sins. As long as your sins are pleasant to look at when gathered in a small group.

This all came home to me this morning when I was in a second hand shop and saw a large plastic tub filled with small baskets. How fitting that the containers are now all together in a larger container. They will not be lonely now. But what about a large plastic container? Shouldn't the baskets we gathered together be placed in a large basket? A large basket with a five foot diameter. A basket the size of the world. It holds all the joys and wonders. Isn't the world just one large basket holding all the cool things and making the solar system sing out with color and symmetry?

About the Book

Welcome to the world of crap you keep instead of throwing out.

It's the stuff that you love to have around you but are not sure why.

There are over fifty essays about the little things in life in this book. Like coloring books and nip bottles. Why do we keep them? Why do we find joy in these things.

There are a variety of items that people collect and decorate their lives with: glass eyes, vomit bags, cardboard music records.

There is a lot of random things that take our fancy and these essays are more celebration than investigation. We get it. You dig what you dig.

From pretty soaps you are not allowed to use to corsages made from dog bones, there is a lot of things we build our history from. This is a little slice of that history.

About the Writer

David is a writer of many things. He has around 150 ebook titles. Now, don't go all impressed on us here. Most of them are pretty damned short. The average length of one of his books is about 65 or 70 pages. His work can be read on the train to work or while you wait for the roast chicken in the over to cook. This book iis a wee bit longer than most of his work, and that's because it was four plus years of work. When you look at each individual column, they pretty darned tiny. David has published short novels such as Delivery, Mr. Lemon Goes Down the List and the Truth Seeker. He has short story collections like Not a Day of Miracles, Some Broken Windows and The Final Girls Support Group's Annual Brownie Bake Off and Other Stories. He also had a series of pop culture essays called the Library of Disposable Art. That's where the column got its name. In that series of short books, David looked at many things such as: The Inner Sanctum movies with Lon Chaney, one episode of the New Scooby Doo Movies, several of the Perry Rhodan German Science Fiction novels and other random shit. David has written several hybrid memoirs such as 100 Monsters, My Life in the Frank N Furter Cult, and the aptly named How To Write a Memoir in Three Days: A Memoir. David lives with his family near Worcester.

37310